Cambridge Elements

Elements in Publishing and Book Culture
edited by
Samantha J. Rayner
University College London
Leah Tether
University of Bristol

THE PEOPLE OF PRINT

Eighteenth-Century England

Adam James Smith, *York St John University*
Rachel Stenner, *University of Sussex*
Kaley Kramer, *Independent Scholar*
Helen Williams, *Northumbria University*
Jacob Baxter, *University of St Andrews*
Kate Ozment, *Case Western Reserve University*
Sarah Griffin, *University of York/York Minster Library*
Lisa Maruca, *Wayne State University*
Barbara Crosbie, *University of Durham*
Dominic Bridge, *Newcastle University*
John Hinks, *Birmingham City University*

Shaftesbury Road, Cambridge CB2 8EA, United Kingdom

One Liberty Plaza, 20th Floor, New York, NY 10006, USA

477 Williamstown Road, Port Melbourne, VIC 3207, Australia

314–321, 3rd Floor, Plot 3, Splendor Forum, Jasola District Centre,
New Delhi – 110025, India

103 Penang Road, #05–06/07, Visioncrest Commercial, Singapore 238467

Cambridge University Press is part of Cambridge University Press & Assessment,
a department of the University of Cambridge.

We share the University's mission to contribute to society through the pursuit of
education, learning and research at the highest international levels of excellence.

www.cambridge.org
Information on this title: www.cambridge.org/9781009629454

DOI: 10.1017/9781009629461

© Adam James Smith, Rachel Stenner, and Kaley Kramer *et al.* 2025

This publication is in copyright. Subject to statutory exception and to the provisions
of relevant collective licensing agreements, no reproduction of any part may take place
without the written permission of Cambridge University Press & Assessment.

When citing this work, please include a reference to the DOI 10.1017/9781009629461

First published 2025

A catalogue record for this publication is available from the British Library

ISBN 978-1-009-62945-4 Paperback
ISSN 2514-8524 (online)
ISSN 2514-8516 (print)

Cambridge University Press & Assessment has no responsibility for the persistence
or accuracy of URLs for external or third-party internet websites referred to in this
publication and does not guarantee that any content on such websites is, or will remain,
accurate or appropriate.

For EU product safety concerns, contact us at Calle de José Abascal, 56, 1°, 28003
Madrid, Spain, or email eugpsr@cambridge.org

The People of Print

Eighteenth-Century England

Elements in Publishing and Book Culture

DOI: 10.1017/9781009629461
First published online: September 2025

Adam James Smith, Rachel Stenner, and Kaley Kramer *et al.*

Author for correspondence: Kaley Kramer, kaleyandreakramer@gmail.com

ABSTRACT: This Element profiles understudied figures in the book and print trades of the eighteenth century. With an explicit focus on intervening in the critical history of the trades, this Element profiles seven women and three men, emphasising the broad range of material, cultural, and ideological work these people undertook. It offers a biographical introduction to each figure, placing them in their social, professional, and institutional settings. The Element considers varied print trade roles including that of the printer, publisher, business-owner, and bookseller, as well as several specific trade networks and numerous textual forms. The biographies draw on extensive new archival research, with details of key sources for further study on each figure. Chronologically organised, this Element offers a primer both on individual figures and on the tribulations and innovations of the print trade in the century of national and print expansion.

KEYWORDS: gender, print trades, regionality, eighteenth century, England

© Adam James Smith, Rachel Stenner, and Kaley Kramer *et al.* 2025

ISBNs: 9781009629454 (PB), 9781009629461 (OC)
ISSNs: 2514-8524 (online), 2514-8516 (print)

Contents

	Preface	1
1	Introduction: The People, Publics, and Commerce of Print by Adam James Smith, Rachel Stenner, and Kaley Kramer	2
2	Elizabeth Nutt: Print Trade Matriarch (1666?–1746) by Helen Williams	10
3	John Nicholson and the Auctioning of Copyright (d.1717) by Jacob Baxter	18
4	Catherine Sanger, Publisher in Bartholomew Close (1687–1716) by Kate Ozment	27
5	John White Junior: Printer in the North (1689–1769) by Sarah Griffin	35
6	Selling the Enlightenment: Mary Cooper and Print Culture (1707–1761) by Lisa Maruca	43
7	The 'Indefatigable' Ann Ward, Printer in York (1715/6–1789) by Kaley Kramer	51

8	Anne Fisher (1719–1778): Not Simply a Printer's Wife by Barbara Crosbie	59
9	Sold at the Vestry: John Rippon (1751–1836) and the Hymnbook Trade by Dominic Bridge	66
10	Diversity in the Book Trades: Ann Ireland (1751–1843) of Leicester by John Hinks	74
11	'Laugh when you must, be candid when you can': The Concealed Resistance of the Radical Printer Winifred Gales (1761–1839) by Adam James Smith	82
	List of Abbreviations	91
	Bibliography	92

Preface

The People of Print is a series that profiles understudied figures in the historic book and print trades. It underscores the centrality of people, starting from the premise that the personnel of the book and print trades were the driving force of print culture. Except for a few key figures, the work of the people of print remains insufficiently understood and overshadowed by the scholarly focus on literary and other cultural producers. This is particularly the case in relation to female labour and creativity. This series is conceived as an entry point for researchers and readers needing a concise and accessible introduction to a particular figure. Each volume comprises ten short essays that describe the life, work, and significant achievements or networks of individuals. However, while it necessarily offers an overview, the series is an intervention rather than a comprehensive assessment. Therefore, each volume will feature at least five female figures. In this, the intention of *The People of Print* is to rebalance attention towards occluded, hidden, and neglected female labour, and the archival lacunae around that labour.

1 Introduction: The People, Publics, and Commerce of Print by Adam James Smith, Rachel Stenner, and Kaley Kramer

The eighteenth-century transformation of the print trade is inseparable from the startling transformations that took place over the course of the century in Britain, and, for this book's purposes, England specifically. These social, legal, and economic developments produced a highly self-aware print culture keen to promote an image of itself as a cornerstone of emerging national values at home and abroad. However, that image often marginalised the histories and subjectivities of groups beyond its male, middling, white, educated mould. While studies of readers and writers have flourished into nuanced perspectives on the complex nature of these activities, work on the diversity of people involved in the print trades is less common. In a century of intense public wrangling over the nature of copyright, the morality of publishing, and the role of print in a rapidly changing nation, the people of print were crucial figures of influence and impact.

Like the century before, the eighteenth century in England closed with a radically altered set of political and economic frameworks from those with which it had begun. Overseas expansion, colonial growth, and final consolidation of 'the United Kingdom' wrought changes to England's self-conception within 'Great Britain' as well as its position on the global stage. These changes, which brought new ideas about nation, citizens, and individuals, developed in tandem with a commercialised society throughout the eighteenth century. Markets were flooded with commodified colonial products, such as chinoiserie and coffee, buoyed on a sea of rampant marketing and publicity, populist politics, and an increasingly 'popular' culture.[1] A dramatic increase in national income took place: during the Glorious Revolution of 1688, the combined income of England and Wales was around £48 million; by the time the fledgling state of Britain incorporated Ireland in 1801, the national income was £232 million.[2]

---

[1] See Mullan and Reid, eds, *Eighteenth-Century Popular Culture*.

[2] Crouzet, 'Toward an Export Economy', p. 78.

Energised by technological advances, cultural change, and increasingly complex internal and external structures, the print trade was one engine in this period of metamorphosis. Mechanisation, as Christopher Flint notes, was crucial: by the end of the eighteenth century, as Clive Siskin argues, it governed the printing processes 'from papermaking to typesetting to the press itself'.[3] The concomitant spread of railways meant that, by the mid-1840s, the dissemination of print was mechanised as well.[4] Practically, print made trade easier, enabling merchants, traders, and entrepreneurs to operate on a scale hitherto unimaginable. It provided a medium for sharing new practices, documenting innovations, debating strategies, and, in theory at least, holding traders accountable. As James Raven notes, 'investors were informed and encouraged by new modes of printed communication; brokers were given new tools to evaluate risk and exchange; agricultural markets were serviced by print stationers; [...] early commercial projects flourished and industrial schemes were organized by document and form'.[5] Printed ledgers, account books, certificates, blank forms, and pocketbooks enabled more consistent and trustworthy bureaucratic and logistic systems. The flurry of documentation also gave rise to new forms of advertisement, which in turn fostered the 'general growth of the service sector in a thriving consumer economy'.[6] In short, as Raven argues, print culture, by 'chronicling, evaluating and instructing, helped effect a business revolution'.[7]

The people of print were a key part of these developments. Print trade professionals, Elizabeth Eisenstein argues, should be viewed as pioneering 'early capitalists'.[8] She characterises the printer as an 'urban entrepreneur' who 'had to recoup large investments and source financial aid; who pioneered in early mass production and extended trade networks [...] who experienced labour problems, including early strikes, and who confronted constant competition from profit driven rival firms'.[9] Guides, manuals, and commentaries explicitly addressed the phenomenon of printing and other technologies. Printing manuals were produced in Europe from the sixteenth

---

[3] See Flint, *Appearance*; Siskin, *Work of Writing*, pp. 11–12.
[4] Siskin, *Work of Writing*, pp. 11–12. [5] Raven, *Publishing Business*, p. 38.
[6] Porter, *Disease*, p. 35. [7] Raven, *Publishing Business*, p. 1.
[8] Eisenstein, *Printing Press*, p. 21. [9] Ibid., p. 21.

century onwards, but their volume increased exponentially in the eighteenth. All of this bespeaks the self-consciousness of the book and print trades and, often, of their products. 'The changes in the eighteenth century were by no means confined to advances in manufacturing', David McKitterick writes; 'they were also changes in outlook, in ways of thinking not just about printing [...] but also about ways by which many other aspects of human activity and knowledge were to be ordered'.[10]

Thus the eighteenth century is often characterised as a period in which the cheaply printed word permeated every facet of what Jürgen Habermas famously termed the bourgeois public sphere. Habermas' formulation is largely based on the accounts of activity recorded in Joseph Addison and Richard Steele's weekly periodical, *The Spectator* (1711–1712).[11] However, periodical historians such as Brian Cowan recognise such publications as, to some extent, works of publicity in and of themselves, explicitly prescribing a vision of coffee house sociability as much as – if not more than – they describe a historical reality.[12] Eighteenth-century print culture did not merely reflect but fashioned the intellectual and social currents of the day.[13] The booming print trade expanded the imagined community of 'the public' that had begun in earlier centuries, inviting readers to imagine themselves as part of a community of well-informed citizens and discerning tastemakers.[14] That community was not, however, restricted to the capital. The urban nexus of print, coffee-houses, and trade in London, all geographically centred on the Royal Exchange, provides a temptingly rich ground for examinations of economy, culture, and regulation. However, while networks of distribution meant that London news circulated widely throughout Britain, regions beyond the capital developed their own audiences and markets, and comparable connections between print trades, coffee-houses, and networks of distribution existed in and between regions throughout the country.

---

[10] McKitterick, *Print*, p. 166.   [11] Habermas, *Structural Transformation*.

[12] Cowan, 'Mr. Spectator', p. 361.

[13] See, for example, Downie and Cornes, ed., *Telling People*.

[14] This is evident in sixteenth-century pamphlet debates. See Shrank, 'Trollers and Dreamers'; Nebeker, 'Broadside Ballad'.

The regional city of York, for example, had a flourishing print trade that was also centred on coffee houses as models of sociable public spaces. 'Coffee Yard', which lies just outside the Minster Gates, had by 1700 been a site of printing for several decades.[15] Lying between Stonegate and Grape Lane, Coffee Lane housed a press and a coffeehouse throughout the eighteenth century. Elsewhere in the city, news and coffee could be had at over thirty coffeehouses that sprang up in quick succession: Sunton's Coffee House on Coney Street hosted the gatherings of the 'Good Humour Club', a social club for professional men that at one time included Laurence Sterne as well as several printers and booksellers; Farnhill's Coffee-House on Ousegate staged travelling shows; Kidd's Coffee-House, 'next to the George Inn' on Coney Street, became the site of Ann Ward's press and the *York Courant* – and continued to provide a public space for concerts (see Chapter 7). The connections between trade and print that are so apparent in studies of eighteenth-century London are equally evident outside of the capital and shaped regional and local public spheres.

The vision of public life conducted in the bustling coffee shops is not, though, as egalitarian as it might at first sound. Brian Cowan explains that 'the coffee-house is portrayed as a social space dedicated to high-minded discourse on a wide range of affairs; it is also assumed to be open to any *man* who wanted to participate in the discussions conducted therein, regardless of social rank'.[16] Periodicals tend to describe the public sphere as being predominantly urban, white, bourgeois, and male – and they frequently assume that readers meet these criteria. Take, for example, the first number of *The Spectator* (1711), a periodical orchestrated by Joseph Addison and Richard Steele.[17] Here Addison writes as the paper's fictional editor, Mr Spectator. He posits that a reader will assess a writer by deducing their identity, particularly, their race, gender, social standing, and marital status:

> I have observed, that a Reader seldom peruses a Book with
> Pleasure 'till he knows whether the Writer of it be a black or
> a fair Man, of a mild or cholerick Disposition, Married or

---

[15] Sessions and Sessions, *Printing in York*, p. 24. [16] Cowan, 'Mr. Spectator', p. 345.
[17] See Ellis, 'Sociability'.

> a Batchelor, with other Particulars of the like nature, that conduce very much to the right Understanding of an Author.'[18]

As Mr Spectator proceeds to assure his readers that he is a property-owning gentleman of some standing, the hierarchy implicitly underpinning this catalogue of characteristics becomes clear. Mr Spectator simultaneously draws the character of the reader, repeatedly complementing 'his' discerning judgement. For instance, he explains, 'I have given the Reader just so much of my History and Character, as to let him see I am not altogether unqualified for the Business I have undertaken'.[19] As Kathleen Wilson argues, 'the national community constructed by the newspaper and the periodical press [was] imagined to consist of free, flourishing, and largely, though not exclusively, white male British subjects'.[20] The existence of 'women, slave and free Africans, Jews, servants, Catholic, labourers, and so on' was barely registered, and could at best be 'extrapolated through the claims made by the male middling sorts or their betters'.[21] This stratified notion of who mattered characterised the growth of Georgian culture, which was, as Pat Rogers points out, 'dictated by the consumerism of the few as much as the commercialism of the many'.[22] Combined with the inference that the reader must be of the male middling sorts, a 'logic of sameness' is discernible in eighteenth-century publications.[23] Such a logic obscures or even erases any subjectivities beyond this narrowly prescribed vector of identity. Since periodicals provided the source material for subsequent histories of the period's print culture, this early omission of identity groups outside white, male, and middle has had a significant and distorting impact on the narrative of who print personnel actually were.

Habermas' foundational account of the emergence of the public sphere is now subject to extensive qualifications and counter-arguments.[24] Rachel Carnell draws attention to Habermas' 'ostensibly universalising humanism',

---

[18] Addison and Steele, *The Spectator*, No. 1, p. 1. [19] Ibid., p. 2.
[20] Wilson, 'Citizenship', p. 73. [21] Ibid. [22] Rogers, *Literature*, p. 6.
[23] Carnell, 'It's not easy', p. 207.
[24] For examples, see Mackie, *Market*; Carnell, 'Protesting', p. 153.

arguing that this impulse has negated attention to historically marginalized groups.[25] Feminist scholarship in particular has addressed the Habermasian model's failures to take account of women's contributions to the literary marketplace. Anthony Pollock and Manushag Powell, for example, each put gender at the centre of their respective projects.[26] In doing so, they foreground the complex ways in which social, discursive, and gender norms interact. Rather than unified standards of social or textual behaviour, print enacted multivalent fictionality and contingent performativity. *The People of Print: Eighteenth Century England* makes a similar adjustment, with reference not to the print that fuelled this public sphere but to the people who produced it.

Established models of the book trade mirror the assumptions of normative masculinity that characterise earlier generations of eighteenth-century scholarship more widely. By focusing on individual lives, this collection adopts micro-history as a method and contributes to the collective endeavour to write a more inclusive printing and publishing history of the period. Here, it joins a groundswell of recent studies which reveal the occluded histories of women of print, overturning long-standing myths about their lack of participation and influence, and promoting new methodologies for doing so.[27] The questions of who these people of print were and even how researchers should define the category 'print personnel' are central to the *People of Print* series, and are the ones we continue broadening with the biographical essays collected here. Micaela Rodgers has recently argued that the Western scholarly reliance on white, hetero, Eurocentric thought and knowledge-production and the power structures embedded within these things have historically discouraged new methods of scholarship within the field of book history.[28] The eighteenth century presents an especially intriguing case study, as this print culture's surviving accounts of itself so explicitly skew towards the male, urban, and bourgeois. This, twinned with galvanisation of the figure of the author as a celebrity figure

---

[25] Carnell, 'Protesting', p. 153. [26] See Pollock, *Gender*; Powell, *Performing*.
[27] See Martinez and Roman, eds, *Female Printmakers*; Wayne, ed., *Women's Labour*; Alexiou et al., eds, *Women in Print*.
[28] Rodgers, 'Deconstructing', p. 517.

during the eighteenth century, has left untold many of the stories of those individuals engaged in the physical, entrepreneurial, and – as Helen Williams argues here – at times domestic labour of producing the printed word (Chapter 2).[29] By focusing on the work of individuals, the commercial networks and social coteries in which they operated and existed, and the decisions they made, this volume, and the series as a whole, furthers David Zaret's assertion that fully understanding the development of print culture necessitates granting 'equal importance to the social and technical aspects of print'.[30] Following this McKenziean paradigm of the sociology of the text, the *People of Print* series directs attention towards the lives, agencies, cultural and political contributions of book, and print trade personnel themselves.

In selecting our case studies, we also continue to counter the historical bias which, as John Hinks argues persuasively, has traditionally privileged London in scholarship on the book and print trades.[31] At the same time, we actively contribute to the recovery of women's work in the trades which, despite recent moves, still remains comparatively neglected. Here, alongside the story of John White Jr (1689–1769), Newcastle's first modern printer (Chapter 5), readers will meet a range of women taking a leading role in the regional trades, such as Anne Ireland (1751–1843), an entrepreneurial printer based in Leicester (Chapter 10); Ann Ward (1716–1789), publisher of *Tristram Shandy* and proprietor of the *Yorkshire Courant* for thirty years (Chapter 7); and Elizabeth Nutt (1666?–1746), a highly networked matriarch of the print trade and the main supplier of news to London from the regions for three decades (Chapter 2). Anne Fisher (1719–1778), based in Newcastle (Chapter 8), and Sheffield's Winifred Gales (1761–1839) (Chapter 11) each offer insights into the varied and active roles undertaken by women. The case of Catherine Sanger (1687–1731), a newly recovered London publisher, showcases the methodological strategies available for reconstructing female agency in the face of archival absence (Chapter 4), while that of Mary Cooper (1707–1761) enables a reassessment of 'trade publishing' and a recovery of her cultural contributions (Chapter 6).

[29] See Griffin, *Authorship*. [30] Zaret, *Origins*, p. 134. [31] Hinks, 'History'.

John Rippon (1751–1836) and John Nicholson (?–d.1717) are included to counter a further bias in book history, identified by Raven, towards literary publishing. 'Non book, or jobbing printing', writes Raven, 'not only supported printers in those periods when they were not printing book, pamphlet and periodical publications, but jobbing itself redefined what was meant by publication'.[32] Jobbing printing might involve 'guides, advice manuals and commentaries [...] printed bills, tickets, receipt forms, commercial and financial blanks, promissory notes, warrants, indentures and authorisations'.[33] In the case of John Rippon, this included hymnodies and related ephemera, for which he successfully created a formidable monopoly while operating from the vestry of his Baptist meeting house (Chapter 9). The chapter on Londoner John Nicholson explores not his life but the curious incident that followed his death: the first documented case of a bookseller's copyrights being sold at auction (Chapter 3).

Like *The People of Print: Seventeenth-Century England*, this collection is a starting point rather than a survey. It recommends new ways of untangling the roles of those print personnel whose lives were so tightly woven into this uniquely prolific print culture: a print culture, which, in publicising a specific version of itself, has so often obscured the agency and labour of the people who made it possible.

---

[32] Raven, *Publishing Business*, p. 8. [33] Ibid.

2 Elizabeth Nutt: Print Trade Matriarch (1666?–1746)
by Helen Williams

2.1 Book Trade Connections

Elizabeth Nutt née Carr (1666?–1746) ran one of the most important wholesale businesses of the early eighteenth-century book trade. Nutt's cluster of shops near the Royal Exchange functioned as the foremost supplier of news to the City of London for three decades.[34] Paula McDowell describes her as one of the 'most influential mercury-women in this period', the others being Anne Dodd and Nutt's and Dodd's daughters.[35] As a mercury, a (usually) female seller of news and ephemera either on the street or from a pamphlet shop, Nutt was a product of a distinct cultural moment: by 1750, mercuries had almost all been replaced by 'newspaper men'.[36] They were significant in being well placed to dodge the law and thereby represent a fully oppositional politics of the period. As Margaret Hunt has demonstrated, mercuries like Nutt paved the way for an enlightened liberal culture of speaking truth to power which provided a foundation for the development of progressive theories of democracy, feminism, and revolutionary politics.[37] Nutt is an interesting exemplar case study of mercury-women in the eighteenth-century book trade partly because the archival record that represents her frequent dealings with the law is so full. Knowing more about her reveals much about women's relationships and business networks in the period as well as the fine line between business and family in enterprises like the Nutts'.

While little is known about Nutt's birth and early years, Margaret Hunt has charted her remarkable rise in the historical record from mercury (newspaper or pamphlet seller) to patented law printer and bookseller.[38] Nutt worked as a mercury before her marriage to printer John Nutt in 1692. This marriage combined her networks and expertise with his technological skills and apparatus, and enabled Nutt to become a printer as well as a seller of books. They set up home and work in the Savoy, off the Strand, in 1705.

---

[34] McDowell, *Grub Street*, pp. 56, 26. [35] Ibid., p. 56.
[36] Hunt, 'Hawkers, Bawlers', pp. 63, 64. [37] Ibid., p. 41. [38] Hunt, 'Nutt'.

In their eighteen years of marriage, they had thirteen children, many of whom became part of the family business.[39] After John's death in 1716, Nutt printed and published works under her own name, before sharing the family law patent with her second son, Richard Nutt, from 1722. Nutt produced everything from cheap print to legal tomes, including the *Historia Placitorum* (1736), which Warren M. Billings describes as 'a singular, exquisitely beautiful example of the English printer's craft' in its careful combination of materials, typography, and design.[40]

Nutt collaborated with the leading women of the eighteenth-century book trade. Through a partnership with Anne Dodd (d.1739), Nutt also acquired a reputation for selling cheap nonfiction, mostly bawdy or sensationalist works, which engaged with the religious, political, and proto-feminist ideas of the moment.[41] Their joint imprint is attached to over 130 titles published from the 1720s until Nutt's death in 1746, with Hunt remarking that 'there are few more ubiquitous names on the title pages of books of this period than those of Dodd and Nutt'.[42] Nutt also participated in a female conger (bookselling syndicate), which included Dodd, Ruth Charlton, Mary Cooke, and J. Read, to produce the expensive *Annotations on the Holy Bible* in 1735.[43]

Hunt has claimed that Dodd and Nutt seemed to own controlling interests in one or more of the leading opposition journals of the 1720s and 1730s, and that the participation of mercuries in newspaper-owning congers would have given those enterprises a stronger chance of success. Their experience in newspaper distribution gave them easy and possibly cut-price access to cross-advertising opportunities in papers with significant circulation (of up to tens of thousands of copies in some cases): 'Indeed in the decade and a half between 1720 and 1735 the mercuries actually appear for a short time to have gained a competitive edge over the majority of the male booksellers'.[44]

As she was extremely well connected, a study of Nutt sheds light on the depth and intricacies of book trade networks, the degree to which women were key to the success of family businesses, and how the expertise of the

---

[39] Ibid. [40] Billings, 'A Neglected Treatise', p. 281, n. 65. [41] Hunt, 'Nutt'.
[42] Hunt, 'Hawkers, Bawlers', pp. 49–50. [43] Ibid., p. 49. [44] Ibid., pp. 49–50.

mercury was a distinct advantage in early eighteenth-century publishing. The rest of this chapter deals with her involvement in an oft-cited moment in book trade history – the Persian Libel crisis of 1728. A closer look at the manuscripts comprising the documentary record of the crisis helps to contextualise Nutt's role as a matriarch of the early eighteenth-century book trade in a manner extending beyond her own immediate family business.

2.2 Women in the State Papers

Nutt has captivated scholars because of her remarkable presence in the State Papers, where she frequently appears as a proponent of an opposition press during the period of Whig supremacy under Robert Walpole that became known as the Robinocracy (roughly 1721–1742). It is difficult to know whether this was as a result of a strong political belief on her part or down to a commercial decision to position herself as a producer of politically and/or ecclesiastically dissident print, which could be lucrative.[45] Nutt's printed output reveals that she moved smoothly between radical Whig and Tory output. As Hunt warns, we should take care to avoid jumping to conclusions about Nutt's political identity.[46] Her son Richard, however, was accused of having 'barely concealed Jacobite tendencies'.[47]

Given her penchant for producing work frequently perceived to be on the wrong side of the law, Nutt's large family contributed to her success and survival, and to the growth of a periodical empire that in turn brought her more often into conflict with the state. Her son Richard became the printer of the *London Evening-Post*, an opposition paper. As a seller of that as well as the *Craftsman* (an anti-Walpole periodical) and *Mist's Weekly Journal* (a Jacobite weekly), Nutt and her family were frequently arrested for the dissemination of anti-government propaganda, becoming known for radical – and often illegal – print material.[48] Nutt's daughters Catherine, Alice, and possibly Sarah, who helped her to manage several bookshops or bookselling outlets across London, often covered for each other.[49] When Nutt went into hiding after a 1729 issue of the *Daily Post*

---

[45] Ibid., p. 44. [46] Ibid., p. 56. [47] Ibid., p. 55. [48] Hunt, 'Nutt'.
[49] McDowell, *Grub Street*, p. 56; Hunt, 'Hawkers, Bawlers', p. 53.

prompted arrests, her daughter Catherine claimed that she was in Bath and explained that she and her sister Alice were trusted to manage the shop and trade in her absence.[50]

Nutt's role as the head of a network, or what McDowell would call 'economic family', meant that her business was resilient. As McDowell puts it,

> to see fellow tradesmembers [...] taking on additional chores when one or more of their co-workers was in custody, is to sense the guild-like solidarity of these interdependent workers, and the efficient redistribution of human resources that took place in response to disruption from outside.[51]

The solidarity and endurance of family-based networks and the advantages of group action are well evidenced in the ways Nutt's daughters were able to interchangeably operate outlets of the Nutt enterprise. As Hunt has argued, the frequency with which we see female opposition publishers featuring in the State Papers demonstrates that husband–wife or printer–daughter/sister relationships could function as a business strategy enabling printers and publishers to continue the family business while one person was imprisoned or in hiding.[52] The recording of these circumstances in the State Papers is one of the primary means of becoming privy to the family structures of the book trade in this period.[53]

Perhaps the most important source on Nutt, because it appears as a self-representation in manuscript, is her request for a *nolle prosequi* (dismissal of legal proceedings) in response to her arrest for publishing a libellous issue of *Mist's Weekly Journal*. McDowell has described Nutt crafting an image for herself here 'as a matriarch of the London pamphlet trade'.[54] Writing in the third person, Nutt describes herself as 'an Antient Woman, near seventy

---

[50] Delafaye, 'Examination'; see also McDowell, *Grub Street*, p. 101.
[51] McDowell, *Grub Street*, p. 71.   [52] Hunt, 'Hawkers, Bawlers', pp. 50, 54.
[53] For a discussion of this dynamic in a later period, see Gardner, *Business of News*.
[54] McDowell, *Grub Street*, p. 105.

years of Age', at the head of a 'Numerous Family'. Deploying the typical defence of ignorance, she alleges 'That she has [...] at all times to the best of her knowledge avoided giving Offence to the Government' while giving 'all the Information she could' about her fellows in trade.[55] Nutt was experienced in dealing with these situations, being a leader in opposition publishing, and in printing, publishing, and disseminating works that demanded political accountability. While many book trade wives appearing in the State Papers claim ignorance of the contents of the papers they printed or sold, Nutt's status and impact in the trade should have meant that, in McDowell's words, 'claiming naiveté was not an option'.[56] Nutt had been widowed for twelve years by this point. And such was her reputation – accrued through frequent appearances before officials for similar offences – that bail amounts for Nutt were 'almost always higher than for everyone else involved in a given publication', even compared to printers.[57] Nutt persevered in claiming innocence even when she considered it unlikely that she would be believed, a strategic move which may in context have been interpreted as a sarcastic acknowledgement of her commitment to remain silent.

2.3 The 1728 Raid on Mist's Weekly Journal

The context for Nutt's arrest sheds light upon the world over which she reigned as matriarch and the blurred lines between family and business. *Mist's Weekly Journal* was a Jacobite periodical that frequently walked a fine line on the verge of sedition. In 1728, the journal suffered what Matthew Thomas Symonds has called 'the Persian libel crisis'.[58] A piece on Persia had been published on 24 August that prompted complaints from Hampton Court to the Lord Chancellor, insisting that the paper had taken 'Treason and Insolence [...] beyond any Instance that perhaps has ever been known of the like nature'.[59] The offending piece was a letter signed by 'Amos Dudge', a pseudonym of Philip, first Duke of Wharton, presenting the overthrow of a rightful Persian emperor and the people's subsequent

---

[55] Nutt, 'Petition to be discharged'; see also McDowell, *Grub Street*, p. 105.
[56] McDowell, *Grub Street*, p. 105. [57] Ibid., p. 70.
[58] Symonds, 'Grub Street Culture', p. 2. [59] Anon., 'From Hampton Court'.

dissatisfaction.[60] It was an extreme case, using allegory to attack George II and Sir Robert Walpole and praise the Pretender James III. Being a 'Persian letter', the piece appeared as a credible item of 'news', capitalising on the paper's tendency to print updates from that part of the world.[61] But this was also a literary construct which had become popular since Charles de Secondat, Baron de Montesquieu's satirical *Persian Letters* (1722), and in this case probably chosen in the awareness that allegory made legal prosecution more challenging.[62] This was by no means a standard issue of *Mist's Journal*: its producers had anticipated the letter's popularity. It was recognised at the time that 'great numbers were sold', a number which has since been claimed to be 10,750 copies.[63] The Persian libel was an eighteenth-century bestseller which required forward planning and an expansive network of willing accomplices.

His Majesty's Messengers in Ordinary were promptly sent to search the printing house and arrest all concerned. The arrests as such were not unusual in themselves but notable in scale.[64] The messengers discovered the incriminating copy in Mr Rowe's room, and the formes were believed to have been removed to another printer's – one Mr Barber on Labour in Vain Hill near Blacksmith Hall.[65] Printer William Burton had already been identified as lending his press to the undertaking. Mist and Wharton were in hiding, in France, and Anne Dodd had absconded, but many who had been involved were arrested. Those making the arrest, Samuel Crew, John Hutchins, and Thomas Bincham, described the process in detail in their claim for expenses, emphasising the number of prisoners and the additional costs incurred in preventing their 'Corresponding, or making their Escape'.[66]

---

[60] Symonds, 'Grub Street Culture', p. 265. [61] Ibid.
[62] Black, 'An Underrated Journalist', p. 29. On allegory and the law, see Bricker, *Libel*.
[63] Anon., 'H.M. to Townshend'; Limouze, 'Nathaniel Mist's Weekly Journals', p. 13.
[64] Hunt, 'Hawkers, Bawlers', p. 53. [65] Anon., 'H.M. to Townshend'.
[66] Crew et al., 'Applying'.

Their account of the scale of the arrests is supported by a handwritten 'List of Prisoners', some names from which have featured in McDowell's and Hunt's work on women in the book trades, demonstrating Nutt's participation in an enabling print network.[67] Among the names of Mist's employees, Elizabeth Dodd – as a 'mercury' – is ninth on the list; William Hewer, 'Mrs Dod's [*sic*] man', is tenth. Another list was made 'by Recollection', which additionally included the names of Mary Carter and Eliza Carter, wife and daughter of Mist's apprentice, and Mrs Brett, the wife of one of the publishers. Taken together, the lists describe a network of twenty-five people, including men, women, and children.

Just as informative as the names are the annotations to the lists, which illuminate the socio-economic status of the prisoners and of the complex ways in which gender, age, and labour intersected in the eighteenth-century book trade. The poverty of the scene is laid bare. Crew, Hutchins, and Bincham complained that for 'Thos. Randall and James Foord the two Devill Boys, who was almost naked, we were under necessity, to lay out Fifty shillings upon them or our houses would have been over run with Vermin'.[68] The implication here is that – in addition to being inadequately clothed – they were infested with lice. Randall is the 'good devil', the informer on Burton (and it is tempting to wonder whether this was by accident, in response to poor treatment, or on the promise of 25 shillings worth of new clothes), while Ford, the 'bad devil', is considered 'below punishment'.[69] Even more senior team members did not seem to be thriving. Publisher James Wolfe and his wife are so poor that the messengers noted that her freedom would be the severer punishment, while Wolfe himself remains in custody. Doctor Gaylard, a failed printer-publisher who had returned to work for Mist, was guilty by association, having 'been in the house with' Elizabeth Nutt's agent, and was poor enough to have to provide his own recognizance.[70]

Publishers, on the other hand, were deemed financially secure enough for commitment to be a punishment: mercuries Nutt and Smith, Nutt's

---

[67] Anon., 'A Libel'. The full list is available at the Virtual Museum of Printing website.

[68] Crew et al., 'Applying', f. 99. [69] Anon., 'Two documents'.

[70] Anon., 'A Libel'; Limouze, 'Doctor Gaylard's', pp. 97–103.

agent Anne Neville, and William Hewer, Anne Dodd's man. And so too were the domestic workers that supported these book trade households. Amie Walker, Mist's housekeeper, was committed in the same terms as the mercuries, for 'publishing'. Burton's printing staff – his workman, John Garrer, and his apprentice, Thomas Graham – and Alice Nutt, listed as Nutt's daughter but already identified elsewhere in the State Papers as a cog in the Nutt machine, are dealt with in the same terms as Samuel Duke, Burton's servant, and Judith Salmon, Smith's maid: bailed and able to provide their own recognizances. The counterpart list, 'by Recollection', reveals that Mrs Brett, wife of the publisher, and Mary Carter, wife of Mist's apprentice, were also dealt with in this way. Carter's role was to '[take] care of Mist's house'. Her daughter Eliza was discharged, perhaps because she was considered too young to be involved.[71] Despite not directly working in the book trade, the female domestic staff and Burton's male servant are considered by the messengers to be trade-adjacent, facilitating the publication of libellous print.

2.4 Domestic Labour

Nutt's status as matriarch is particularly important for our understanding of book trade networks in the early eighteenth century. Through striving to better understand her place within the early eighteenth-century book trade, we can also get a better sense of the liminal spaces occupied by other workers. In the case of the Persian libel crisis, all labour in the book trade household was book trade labour. Housekeepers, servants, and maids were treated like wives and grown-up daughters, that is, assumed to be consciously aiding and abetting the publication of libellous print even if they were not employed for that specific purpose. This is the world in which Nutt thrived, making use of women's labour, female kin, and friendships to operate an opposition press from within the grey areas of 'official' print practice.

---

[71] Anon., 'Two documents'.

3 John Nicholson and the Auctioning of Copyright (d.1717) by Jacob Baxter

3.1 Under the Hammer

John Nicholson (d.1717) enjoyed a successful career in the London book trade. After finishing his apprenticeship under Thomas Flesher in 1695, Nicholson had established a shop of his own at the King's Arms in Little Britain by the end of 1698.[72] By the time of his death in May 1717, he had published over three hundred different editions, according to the ESTC, and built up an estate worth around £8,000.[73] This chapter is concerned with one of the final business decisions that Nicholson took. At the end of his will, which was made a month before his death, Nicholson stated that the booksellers Timothy Goodwin and Robert Knaplock should 'supervise the sale' of 'his books and copies', with all money raised going to his estate.[74] Most were eventually sold at two separate auctions. The first took place at four o'clock in the afternoon on 14 April 1718 at the Queen's Head Tavern on Paternoster Row.[75] The second occurred in the same place almost exactly a year later, at three o'clock in the afternoon on 30 March 1719.[76]

By 1718, auctions had been a common fixture in the English print trade for decades. Thousands of books, from hundreds of private libraries, had gone under the hammer since the first known British book auction, which had taken place almost half a century earlier.[77] Nicholson himself had been involved in these sorts of sales, including the auctioning of Sir John Trenchard's library in November 1695.[78] Yet, as far as we can tell, no rights to print a particular work, or copyrights, had ever been auctioned until Nicholson's went up for sale. It is the first such occasion from which a printed catalogue has survived.

---

[72] Mckenzie, *Stationers' Company*, p. 59, no. 1575.
[73] Nicholson's funeral took place on 15 May 1717 (Jones and Holmes, eds., *London Diaries*, p. 674).
[74] 'Will of John Nicholson', f. 238r. [75] Anon., *Queen's Head [. . .] April, 1718.*
[76] Anon., *Queen's Head [. . .] March, 1718.*
[77] Munby and Coral, *British Book Sale*, pp. 3–29.
[78] Nicholson, *Catalogue*, title page.

Many more would follow Nicholson's example. Over the course of the next fifty years, at least 187 copyright auctions (on average, three a year) took place in London, each accompanied by a catalogue. These sales have attracted the attention of book historians before. In 1950, Cyprian Blagden surveyed the Longman Collection, a set of 167 trade catalogues that can currently be found in the British Library.[79] Almost quarter of a century later, Terry Belanger used the copyright catalogues to trace just exactly who owned the right to publish a selection of titles over several decades.[80] He ended with the following reflection:

> Clearly these catalogues [of copyright auctions] should be made more accessible than they now are. What we need is a facsimile of those pages of the catalogues which list copyrights, together with an explanation of the listings ... and most of all, indexes by author, title, buyer, and seller. I have begun work on this formidable undertaking, but since the project will take some time ... it may be useful here to point out that both the Ward and Longman catalogues are available on microfilm from their owners.[81]

Such a volume, as envisaged by Belanger, has thus far not appeared. Moreover, many of the extant catalogues that accompanied copyright auctions in eighteenth-century London remain, by today's standards, inaccessible. Only a handful have been digitised. Nevertheless, developments in book history in the fifty years since Belanger's clarion call, especially within the realm of digital humanities, have helped to make his proposed 'undertaking' less 'formidable'. In particular, the high quality of English national bibliography for the eighteenth century has made it relatively straightforward to match the individual entries in the copyright catalogues to specific editions. By focusing on the two auctions of Nicholson's copyrights, this

---

[79] British Library shelfmark Longman Collection: General Reference Collection C.170.aa.1; Blagden, 'Booksellers'.
[80] Belanger, 'Booksellers', pp. 281–302; Kempis, *Christian's Pattern*.
[81] Belanger, 'Booksellers', p. 297.

chapter illustrates this process, along with the useful findings that can emerge from it.

3.2 The Rules of Play

Before 1660, the right to publish a particular title was usually held by one or, less frequently, two individuals. This offered substantial rewards should a book sell well but also potential bankruptcy if it flopped. After 1660, members of the London book trade began to divide copyrights into ever smaller shares. For instance, as Giles Mandelbrote has shown, the bookseller Richard Bentley (1645–1697) accumulated a plethora of different copyrights in various sizes during a career that spanned almost four decades.[82] Of the 380 titles that he owned at his death, Bentley only held a third in their entirety. The rest were mostly twelfths, thirds, and sixths of other works, as well as smaller shares, including a forty-eighth in a multi-volume dictionary. This segmentation of copyrights helped to reduce risk levels in the London print industry by spreading potential losses among shareholders. Up until February 1774, when the House of Lords voted in favour of Alexander Donaldson in his landmark case against Thomas Becket, the right to publish was, in effect, owned in perpetuity.[83] This meant that transfers in the ownership of a particular text usually came about through one of three ways: gifts, bequests, and sales. These did not always take place with the assistance of the auctioneer. In 1718, the same year as the first known copyright auction in London, the prominent bookseller Jacob Tonson sold all of his copyrights to his nephew for £2,597 16s 8d.[84] This amount eclipsed the combined total raised from both sales of Nicholson's copyright (£232 10s and £1,801, respectively).

The rules underpinning the copyright auctions reflected the cash-poor conditions of the London print trade. The catalogue for the first auction of Nicholson's titles made clear that those who won the right to print a particular work had to either pay in 'ready money' (that is, cash) or provide security for a payment within six months of the sale.[85] When it

---

[82] Mandelbrote, 'Richard Bentley', pp. 77–94. [83] Ibid., p. 55; Rose, 'Author', p. 51.
[84] Tonson, 'Assignment'. [85] Anon., *Queen's Head [...] April, 1718*, p. 1.

came to the second auction, this time limit was reduced to three months.[86] The catalogue for this occasion also made clear that booksellers who bought works that were either being printed or about to go to press had to take on the subsequent costs of their publication. These potentially high upfront costs favoured wealthy and established members of the London book trade.

As the following lots from the second auction indicate, the detail contained within both catalogues is rich:

Knaplock	20. Danet's Dictionary, 4°	A Third.	*1:1:0*
Gosling	21. Treatise of Sea Laws, 4°	A Third.	*12:12:0*
Danlin	22. of Trade, 4°	A Third.	*6:0:0*
Taylor	23. Blome's Bible, with cuts	333 in 1500	*19:15:0*[87]

Each lot entry typically contained, in print, the name of the author, the title of the work, the number of volumes (if there was more than one), the format of the book, and the share size up for sale. Subsequent manuscript additions also denoted how much each lot went for, if they were sold, and who bought them. The first sale of Nicholson's copyrights was made up of eight collections of copyright, grouped together under the names of their previous owners. For instance, Nicholson owned a third of 'all the copies formerly belonging to Mr Robert Clavel', who had passed away either in or just before 1712.[88] This comprised twenty-five named titles, along with other unnamed 'parts and shares of copies'. When he had bought these 'copies', Nicholson had obtained segments of titles that had already been previously divided. For example, either in or just after 1696, he had acquired an eighth of Thomas Basset's copies. Basset had owned a quarter share in *Of the Lawes of Ecclesiastical Politie* (1594) by Richard Hooker in folio and, in 1682, he had co-published an edition of this work with Robert Scot, John Wright, and Richard Chiswell.[89] Because he only bought an eighth of Basset's copies, Nicholson ended up with a thirty-second share in Hooker's most famous work. In April 1718, it went up for sale, as part

---

[86] Anon., *Queen's Head [...] March, 1718*, p. 1.
[87] Anon., *Queen's Head [...] April, 1718*, p. 2. [88] Ibid., p. 6.
[89] Hooker, *Works* (1682).

of a wider portfolio of Basset's copies. At the auction, they were all purchased by Robert Knaplock for £41. He co-published a new edition *Of the Lawes of Ecclesiastical Politie* in 1723.[90] Sixteen booksellers were involved with the publication this time.

The first sale of Nicholson's copyright harked back to an older way of doing things. Various portions of his literary property were put up for sale in large tranches. The second auction presented a new approach, with ninety lots of mostly individual titles. The works listed in the catalogue for this auction were varied in terms of genre, including works of history, classical texts, philosophy, and natural sciences.[91] Equally diverse were the shares on offer. As Table 1 demonstrates, the majority of share sizes fell down conventional routes, divided between groups of two, three, or four publishers, or not at all. Nicholson owned few titles in their entirety. Other entries in the catalogue indicate scenarios where Nicholson had, at some point, increased his stake (such as the two-sevenths or five-sixths sized shares). Some of the shares with large denominators (such as 333/2000) were likely dictated by the envisaged print run for the book. Accurate recording of the various shares was a source of some concern, as a cautious note in the second auction catalogue suggests:

> The several parts and shares of copies throughout the whole, according to the best information can be got, are true and exact. However, everyone is at liberty before the sale to satisfy themselves of any of those shares, the executors undertaking to sell no more nor no other title, than what Mr Nicholson had when he died, which are supposed and believed to be the same as mentioned in the following list.[92]

The Register of the Stationers' Company may have offered one way of tracing the shares, although its regulatory power had been diluted with the passing of the Statute of Anne in 1710.[93] As the eighteenth century wore on,

---

[90] Hooker, *Works* (1723).
[91] Anon., *Queen's Head [. . .] March, 1718*, pp. 2–3; lots 34, 39, 44, and 62.
[92] Ibid., p. 1. [93] Gadd, 'Stationers', p. 87.

Table 1 The frequency of copyright shares in the second Nicholson sale

Share Size	Number of Titles
1/3	18
1/2	14
1/4	13
1/16	10
1/8	6
Whole	6
Unspecified	4
1/6	4
1/5	2
1/40	1
1/9	1
2/7	1
222/2000	1
231/1000	1
233/1500	1
3/8	1
333/1500	1
333/2000	1
333/3000	1
389/1250	1
444/2000	1
5/6	1

the copyright catalogues themselves became more important for identifying who had the right to print a particular title – one reason why these ephemeral publications survived.

3.3 The Purchasers

An estimate of the attendance at both auctions can be gauged by the number of buyers listed, assuming that they all represented themselves. For instance, the ninety lots at the second Nicholson auction were sold among thirty different individuals. The prices for which copyrights were sold at these auctions ranged from £10s 6d for half of the right to publish an English translation of Tacitus, to hundreds of pounds, with religious works typically attracting the biggest sums.[94] In March 1719, two shares, each of an eighth, in the sermons of John Tillotson went for £250 each to James Round and John Pemberton, making up nearly a quarter of the total money raised in the second sale.[95]

According to the ESTC, at least seventy-five of the ninety-three (80%) titles listed in the second catalogue can be matched to a 'pre-sale' edition that carries Nicholson's name. Out of the seventy-three titles that were sold from the same catalogue, thirty-eight (51%) 'post-sale' editions can be identified; that is, editions printed after the date of the auction that includes the purchaser's name in the imprint. The interval between pre- and post-sale editions could be brief. For example, Round and Pemberton had produced a new edition of Tillotson's sermons by the end of 1720.[96] They were evidently keen to begin making back the money that they had spent. In other instances, no new edition from the purchaser can be identified. This could be due to loss, or to the fact that, along with the right to print the book, the bookseller had received a number of unsold copies at the auction as well.

A few patterns emerge from scrutinising the buyers present at the sales of Nicholson's copyrights. One is that some booksellers, as in the case of Arthur Bettesworth, went to the auctions to increase the share that they already had in a certain title. Bettesworth bought Nicholson's share in the *Exercitia Latina*, a schoolbook that he had already helped to publish three years earlier.[97] Another pattern is that when the same works came up in

---

[94] Anon., *Queen's Head [. . .] March, 1718*, p. 1, lot 1.   [95] Ibid., p. 2, lots 9 and 10.
[96] Tillotson, *Works*.
[97] Anon., *Queen's Head [. . .] March, 1718*, p. 4, lot 78; Anon., *Exercitia Latina* (1716); *Exercitia Latina* (1720).

consecutive lots, booksellers had to be prepared for a fluctuation in price. For instance, the fourth lot of the second Nicholson auction, which offered a sixteenth share in two dictionaries by John Harris (the *Lexicon Technicum* and *Glossographia Anglicana*), was bought by Benjamin Cowse for £40. The fifth lot contained the same titles and went, for the same price, to the same person. But when it came up for a third time in the sixth lot of the sale, Cowse had to pay £49. He eventually published a new edition of the *Lexicon Technicum* in 1723.[98]

3.4 Cartelisation

The battle over the *Lexicon Technicum* was a rare moment of tension in a likely docile affair. Other copyright catalogues hint at a fairly convivial atmosphere. The catalogue outlining the copies that belonged to Awnsham Churchill, which were auctioned in August 1720, promised on its title page that at one o'clock 'the company will be entertained with a good dinner'.[99] Few other occasions, with the exception of funerals and meetings of the Stationers' Company, would attract so many booksellers under one roof. This was, nevertheless, a closed world and it seems unlikely that copyright catalogues were circulated to a wider audience. A catalogue printed in 1767 made clear on its title page that the copies would 'be sold by auction to a select number of the booksellers of London and Westminster'.[100] Copyright auctions were designed to entrench existing oligopolies, rather than open the print industry to new competitors.

Even with just two catalogues, which outline the copyrights that had formerly belonged to John Nicholson, a huge amount of information can be ascertained about the ownership of printed matter in early eighteenth-century England. They provide a glimpse into the finances of publishers and shed further light on how much money was required for the production of a printed book. They bring a relative degree of order to the chaotic cartelisation that engulfed the London book trade in the decades either side of the eighteenth century. Nicholson himself was not afraid of taking risks during his career. In 1698 he took the relatively unusual step of organising

[98] Harris, *Lexicon Technicum*. [99] Anon., *Queen's Head [. . .] July, 1720*.
[100] Anon., *Catalogue [. . .] Jacob and Richard Tonson*, p. 1.

a lottery to sell over a thousand law books.[101] But it was one of the final gambles of his career that would result in his most lasting legacy. His request for his copies to be posthumously sold off resulted in an innovation, which allows us to reconstruct, in some detail, the otherwise murky world of eighteenth-century copyright.

---

[101] Anon., *New Adventure*.

4 Catherine Sanger, Publisher in Bartholomew Close (1687–1716) by Kate Ozment

Catherine Sanger (active 1713–1717) was a publisher in London who sold literary and religious texts with her husband, Egbert Sanger. Catherine has, until this article, been rendered invisible by a combination of limited traces of her labour, assumptions of masculinity, and scholarly disinterest. This profile details Sanger's life and contributions to English print history and the methods through which her contributions were recovered as a model for future work.

4.1 The Life of Catherine Sanger

Catherine Shalcross was baptised on 17 July 1687 at St. Martin-in-the-Fields in Westminster. Her parents were Henry, a lawyer who died in 1697, and Abigail Shalcross, whose origins are less clear. I cannot find information about Catherine's early life in London, but she was the child of a lawyer and gentleman and might have had a typical upbringing for her station. She appears again in May 1711 when she married Egbert Sanger in St. Giles in the Fields in Holborn. Egbert was baptised in St. Paul's on 2 July 1684 by his parents, Edward, a tailor, and Susana Sanger. Egbert and Catherine had one child, also Catherine, who was baptised on 29 February 1711/12.

Egbert was a publisher and bookseller who was apprenticed in the Stationers' Company to Mary Tonson in 1699. His imprints in the ESTC detail a career extending from his freedom in 1707 to November 1712, when he died at twenty-eight years old. The Sanger shop was located at the Post House near the Middle Temple Gate in Fleet Street, and Egbert averaged twenty publications a year. Egbert's titles share space with well-known figures in the book trades including the Tonsons and Edmund Curll, and he frequently published literary works including poetry and drama alongside topical pamphlets covering religion and politics. Given his status as a Stationer, connections to the Tonsons and Curll, and publication of significant figures like John Dryden and William Shakespeare, Egbert is decently documented.[102] Catherine, on the other hand, has remained in relative obscurity.

Despite its brevity, Catherine's career after Egbert's death is interesting for the ways it makes visible otherwise untracked familial ties between booksellers in the trades. According to an advertisement in *The Daily Courant* on 23 March 1712/13, four months after Egbert's burial, the stock of the Sanger shop was sold and the space was available for lease. The advertisement reads that 'there is also a Number of valuable Pamphlets, to be Sold very cheap by the Dozen' along with 'a Parcel of Household-Goods' from a house in Boswell Court, near Lincoln's Inn.[103] The stock was bought by three tradespeople: Jonah Brown, William Mears, and John Morphew, all of whom were known for selling pamphlets and other popular literature and would have had a ready market for the imprints that Egbert financed or sold.[104] This is a curious documentary record to find when one is tracing a book trade widow. Inheritances and patrimony were what created the opportunity for many people to enter the trades, especially women who were less likely to be apprenticed as a stationer.[105]

It seems that Catherine did not take the typical route of a widow like Tace Sowle or Elizabeth Nutt, both of whom continued to run the business in the same vein as their deceased spouses. What moves she made can be traced through clues in imprint language and advertisements. Catherine appears on imprints as 'K. Sanger', with the K as an alternate spelling of her name.[106] The name of her business appears on seven books, six in the ESTC and one located through an advertisement in *The Post-Boy* in 1714 (marked with an asterisk). They are as follows:

1. John Oldmixon, *Secret History of Europe*, 1713
2. Thomas Betterton, *The Amorous Widow*, 1714

---

[102] See, for example, Cannan, 'Early Shakespeare Criticism' and Rogers and Baines, 'Edmund Curll'.
[103] 'Advertisements and Notices', *The Daily Courant*, p. 2.
[104] 'Advertisements and Notices', *Evening Post*, p. 3.
[105] See McDowell, *Grub Street*; Mitchell, 'Women'; Hunt, 'Women's Participation'.
[106] In different documents, her name is spelled Catharine, Catherine, and Katherina.

3. William Shakespeare, *The Works of Mr. William Shakespeare*, 1714
4. *Nicolas Boileau Despréaux, *Art of Poetry*, 1714
5. Anonymous, *The Devout Christian's Companion*, 1715
6. M. D'Artanville, *Memoirs of Prince Eugene of Savoy*, 1716
7. John Hughes, *Calypso and Telemachus*, 1717[107]

Not all the imprints have location information included, but when they do, Catherine is identified as operating out of Bartholomew Close. Given that the Sanger shop in Fleet Street was let shortly after Egbert's death along with the sale of the household goods, it is not surprising that Catherine listed a different location. However, it is odd for a widow to give up a shop and lease to set up elsewhere immediately after if she wanted to continue in the trades. Bartholomew Close was a little over a kilometre to the northeast, less immediately in the vicinity of where tradespeople were operating in the 1710s.[108]

Examining the publication history of Catherine's seven titles shows some consistency between her and Egbert's output. Shakespeare, Hughes, Betterton, and *Devout Christian's Companion* were all titles previously published under Egbert's firm. There is a significant overlap in other names on the imprints as well, with Curll and Arthur Bettesworth appearing repeatedly. This suggests that Catherine retained her copyright claims to these books and that they were not sold with the back stock of books and pamphlets. If the copyright was sold, her name would be replaced by Brown, Mears, Morphew, or another tradesperson. This is further supported by the language of these new imprints: it is always 'printed for' Catherine, not 'printed by' or 'sold by'. While early 1700s imprint language cannot be wholly relied upon as an authoritative indication of who completed what labour for a book's production, the consistency suggests that Catherine was financing the books or had copyright claims to them.[109] In

---

[107] The ESTC numbers for all but Boileau are as follows: N36599, T66302, T26042, T164995, N64190, and T19848. They are accessible by searching 'K. Sanger' in the publisher field of the database as of June 2023. Boileau's *Art of Poetry* is likely record T139159, and either the catalogued copy did not have K. Sanger on the imprint or the firm did not appear on the imprint, only in advertisements.

[108] Raven, *Bookscape*, maps 4.1 and 5.3.   [109] Raven, *Publishing Business*.

modern parlance, she would have been a publisher, but that word has different connotations in the early 1700s.[110]

The other three titles are new publications without a direct connection to Egbert's firm.[111] They are similarly characterised as 'printed for' Catherine, indicating financing and not the new establishment of a retail location, which is consistent with her other publications. In a deviation from her other titles, these three are all connected to a new book trade partner: John Darby. Darby was the second of his name to work in the trades, and he had an established business as a printer and bookseller in Bartholomew Close, the same location where Catherine was now listing her publishing business. Furthering the suggestion that there was a connection between these two firms is the newspaper advertisement for *The Art of Poetry*, published in the *Post-Boy* edition for 24–27 July 1714.[112] The copy reads: 'Printed for E. Curll [...] and K. Sanger, at J. Darby's in Bartholomew-Close'. The preposition *at* signals something particularly interesting – that Catherine was operating *in* Darby's shop, not simply running her business in the same courtyard or neighbourhood. This hints at a more intimate relationship than simple business partners, another atypical document for a widow's book trade career. And as it turns out, Catherine and Darby were more intimate than typical business partners. Darby married Elizabeth Shallcrosse on 29 February 1703/4. Elizabeth and Catherine's given names of Shallcrosse and Shalcross are very similar, especially in a period with more phonetic than legalistic spelling norms.[113] It seems that Elizabeth and Catherine were related, and thus John was Catherine's family by marriage.

---

[110] See Treadwell, 'London'; Ozment, 'What Does It Mean to Publish?'

[111] There are some general overlaps. Egbert previously published a different text from Boileau, and Catherine continues to work with Egbert's previous partners on these new ventures as well as the old ones, especially Curll.

[112] 'Advertisements and Notices', *Post Boy*, p. 2.

[113] Unfortunately, their names are common enough that I cannot concretely identify that they have family ties. There are Shallcrosses in most counties in Southern England with their first names in these date ranges. However, I would argue that the details here are too startlingly similar to be a coincidence.

This connection paints a picture of how family ties shaped Catherine's transition from wife to widow in the book trades. Egbert died and left Catherine as a young mother to an infant and widow who had just married into a trade she was not raised in. Given that they were only married a year, perhaps she did not feel equipped to continue the business on her own, especially with a small child. She decided to sell off the bulk of her husband's physical assets – the books, household goods, and retail space – but kept some of her copyright claims and ran a small publishing business out of her family's more established printing firm in Bartholomew Close. This was likely a mutually beneficial relationship. The Darbys allowed Catherine to support herself with fewer overheads, and in turn she employed John as a printer.

Catherine seems to have ceased her business in 1717 and moved to Eton in Berkshire, west of London. She registered her will in June 1731, leaving everything to her only child, Catherine.[114] She does not note any claims to the English stock or other copyright assets but does detail household goods and stock in the South Sea and East India companies. It is perhaps these latter assets that supported Catherine and allowed her to exit trade and live a more retired life. Most of the books for which she was not the publisher were not reprinted in the decades following her retirement, indicating that she let her claims to them lapse.

4.2 Catherine Sanger and the Assumptions of the English Short Title Catalogue

This ends the brief but interesting sketch of Catherine Shalcross Sanger's time in the English book trades. She relied on family ties, as did many stationers, but reshaped her business from what she inherited into something that better fit her abilities and interests. Sanger is also compelling as a case study for how women's labour in the book trades can be obscured or uncovered depending on the interest and values of the bibliographer or cataloguer interpreting data in the ESTC.

---

[114] Will of Catherine Sanger, p. 158 (verso and recto).

Full Record	Permalink
Format options:	Standard format Summary MARC tags HOLDINGS DETAILS
Record 1 out of 1	← Previous record Next record →
ESTC System No.	006220247
ESTC Citation No.	**T19848**
Author - personal	●Hughes, John, 1677-1720.
Title	●Calyp[so] and Telemachu[s.] An opera. Written by Mr. Hugh[es.] The musick compos'd by Mr. Gal[liard.]
Edition	The second edition.
Publisher/year	●London : Printed for K. [sic] Sanger, and sold by A. Dodd at the Peacock without Temple-Bar, 1717.
Physical descr.	vii,[1],64p. ; 8°.
General note	Libretto based on François de Salignac de la Mothe Fénélon's 'Les aventures de Télémaque'.
	Price on title page: (Price One Shilling.)
Surrogates	Microfilm. Woodbridge, Conn. : Primary Source Microfilm, an imprint of Gale Group, 2004. 1 reel ; 35 mm. Unit 420. (The Eighteenth Century ; reel 14699, no. 03).
Subject	●Operas -- Librettos.

Figure 1 ESTC record T19848: Calypso and Telemachus (2nd edn, 1717). ©British Library Board, licenced under CC BY 4.0. Screenshot is from 22 February 2023.

My introduction to Catherine Sanger was through happenstance, on the ESTC record T19848 for the second edition of *Calypso and Telemachus*, an opera by John Hughes (Figure 1). The imprint read, 'Printed for K. [*sic*] Sanger, and sold by A. Dodd at the Peacock without Temple-Bar, 1717' with a bracketed [*sic*] as an editorial addition to indicate that the first initial was a typo.[115] My checks in the *British Book Trade Index* and Plomer's *Dictionary* suggested that the initial was supposed to be an 'E' for Egbert Sanger, who has around 120 imprints in the catalogue.[116] However, a subsequent search of the ESTC revealed that there are six records with the firm name 'K. Sanger', and the initial is never expanded or explained in this space. The ESTC was not clear who this is, but it was not a typo. Given that K. Sanger appeared in 1713, the year that Egbert's 'E. Sanger'

---

[115] This record has since been changed through the author's error report.

[116] Plomer et al., *Dictionary*.

disappeared, it seemed highly likely that K. Sanger represented the work of a child or widow.

Connecting K. Sanger to Catherine Sanger was not particularly difficult in the age of digitized records: she is listed in Egbert's will as executrix, and their marriage license can be viewed on Ancestry.com. In terms of book trade history Catherine's obscurity is understandable in the sense that she was a minor figure, but it is also the result of a gendered history created through centuries of scholarly judgement about what is significant. I believe that this story would have come to light faster if K. had stood for a son rather than a wife, and this belief comes from experience with sexist assumptions going back to Plomer's *Dictionary* that supposes 'A. Dodd' was a *he* and not the prolific Anne Dodd.[117]

These older choices influence contemporary ideologies as well. The public side of the ESTC only traces the last known edit to a record (and it shows when it was edited and by which institution, not what fields are edited). Checking old versions of the ESTC is therefore one of the only reliable ways to broadly date when additions are made. The relatively recent edit to K. Sanger's firm is significant because it was not added with the brackets on the title which do appear in the 2003 edition but by an editor in the last twenty years who took the time to see the record and decide that K. Sanger must be Egbert, presumably because he is otherwise documented and his name is on the first edition of the opera. However, he was deceased for five years by the time this edition came out.

This scenario begs the question of how many nearly untraceable edits to the ESTC are made with the same logic, and how many women are

---

[117] Plomer et al., *Dictionary*, p. 105. The [*sic*] for K. Sanger does not appear in the last pre-Internet edition of the ESTC, which is the third digital edition published via CD-ROM in 2003. My thanks to Brian Geiger for sending me the files for this edition of the ESTC. It does not run on contemporary Windows operating systems, so I used Oracle's VirtualBox to install Windows 98 in a partition on a Windows 10 OS. While dating or tracking different editions of the ESTC may be a niche interest, it is worrisome that the CD-ROMs are almost inaccessible in such a short period of time. Versioning is going to be impossible soon, and researchers will lose the ability to track several decades of ESTC changes.

similarly erased by the default assumption of masculinity. There are more Catherine Sangers to be located. In a short amount of time, my sceptical reading of book trade resources has uncovered Jane Graves, who published under her husband John's imprint of 'J. Graves' for three years after his death. Additionally, biographical research has provided names for Mrs. Amey and the many initials that appear in the 1740s at the same locations: J., E., and M. Amey. These are the marks of Robert and Elizabeth Amey and their children, John, Elizabeth, Margaret, and Matilda. The Women's Print History Project team and forthcoming work from Molly Yarn have identified many more of these examples.[118] While the process of recovering women in the book trades is resource intensive work that will not be easily completed, the prevalence of these examples proves that the assumption that women are marginal in the book trades is more gendered hypothesis than reality.

---

[118] www.womensprinthistoryproject.com; Yarn, 'Invisible'.

5 John White Junior: Printer in the North (1689–1769) by Sarah Griffin

John White Jr. was Newcastle's first modern printer. Throughout his long career, White Jr. demonstrated innovation and collaboration, establishing successful printing businesses in Newcastle and York. He created two long-standing newspapers, the *Newcastle Courant* and the *York Courant*, and showed himself to be a shrewd and astute businessman. Moreover, he had a talent for recognising new business opportunities and creatively managing his relationships with both print networks and legal regulations.

5.1 Pioneering in Newcastle

It is likely that White Jr. was apprenticed to his father, John White Sr., who had been named 'printer for the city of York and the five Northern Counties' by King William and Queen Mary in 1688.[119] He left York, however, and began his career in Newcastle before he was twenty. Aside from purely personal motivations for the move, at least two reasons suggest themselves. White Jr. likely recognised that in York he would be either part of or a direct competitor to his father's press, while White Sr.'s ambitions, following the favour shown to him by William and Mary, may have stretched further than York. Newcastle, which was without an established press or printing culture, was an obvious choice and a city with which White Sr. had some professional connections, having printed at least one Newcastle sermon for Joseph Hall, bookseller on Tyne Bridge, in 1691.

Whatever the motivation, by 1708, John White Jr. was in Newcastle and had set up a printing press.[120] In 1711 he established the *Newcastle Courant* in direct competition to Joseph Button's *Northern Courant*, published in Gateshead. Up to 1716, White Jr.'s publications include at least two reprints of seventeenth-century London printings in 1711, and two original outputs in 1711 and 1712.[121] During these early years, he also attended to his

---

[119] See Sessions and Sessions, *Printing in York*, pp. 24–25.
[120] Gardner, 'John White', p. 73; Crosbie, 'Provincial Purveyors', p. 205.
[121] The reprints were Shirley, *Famous History*; Wigglesworth, *Day of Doom*. The original titles were Anon., *Wit Newly Revived* and Hill, *Ecclesiastes*.

distribution network. On the title page of a book printed in 1710, the imprint reads 'printed and sold by John White, where country chapmen may be furnished with sermons, histories &c.'[122] Chapmen were travelling salesmen and a vital part of the book trade supply network.

At this early stage in his career, White Jr. had a monopoly on the trade in Newcastle, printing on his own for three years. He was, however, at the forefront of a growing industry. During the 1720s and 1730s, only White and two others were printing in the city. This increased to eight by 1740, comparable with York at the same time, and eleven by 1750.[123] Other areas of the book trade in Newcastle were also developing: by the end of the eighteenth century there were over sixty printers, publishers, and booksellers in the city.[124]

The ESTC lists 205 titles over White Jr.'s career. Dates do not appear on his imprints until 1711, however; *Hidden Things Brought to Light*, a twenty-four-page chapbook on how to understand the use of money in the Bible, was likely printed earlier, in 1708, and is the fourth edition of a London title.[125] His final two books, printed during 1769, are a religious tract on the Trinity, and a mathematical work on calculus. This wide range of subjects, from religion to mathematics, is typical of titles coming from White Jr.'s press throughout his long career. Most of White Jr.'s extant output comprises religious tracts and sermons, the stock in trade for many printers; not far behind are broadsheets featuring ballads and poems. He also printed auctioneer's bills and sales catalogues, including catalogues for his own stock, being one of the earliest regional booksellers to do so.[126] John Feather differentiates between those producing newspapers, jobbing printers, and 'printers who really did produce books'.[127] Newspapers and ballads indeed made up a large proportion of White Jr.'s output; however, he did not limit himself to cheaper ephemeral productions. One of his most significant books was the lavishly illustrated *Antiquities of Newcastle* by

---

[122] Anon., *History of Two Children*.
[123] Crosbie, 'Provincial Purveyors', p. 208; Hunt, *Book-trade*, p. 105.
[124] Smith, 'Books and Culture', p. 1.   [125] Axford, *Hidden Things*.
[126] Davies, *Memoir*, p. 236.   [127] Feather, 'Country Trade', p. 166.

Durham-born antiquarian and topographer John Brand, an ambitious and well-received subscription project published in 1767.

5.2 Civic Development and Print Culture

By the beginning of the eighteenth century, Newcastle had recovered significantly from the turmoil of the seventeenth century. Writing in the 1720s, Daniel Defoe found the city a 'spacious, extended, infinitely populous place'; he noted the trades of shipbuilding and iron founding but also the level of poverty.[128] As Newcastle developed, it required and built an improved civic government and infrastructure; its appeal was noted by John Wesley when he wrote in his journal in 1758 that he knew 'no place in Great Britain comparable to it for pleasantness'.[129] This was the environment and community in which White Jr. established himself, and much of the material over his printing career reflects important advances in the making of a modern city. His first such title was printed in 1711 for the Sons of the Clergy, a new charity established for the descendants of clergymen. Their inaugural sermon, preached in St Nicholas church in September of that year, was printed by White Jr., signing himself as 'Printer to the Society'.[130] As more great public buildings appeared, he became the printer of choice, celebrating the Newcastle infirmary in 1753, and a Lying-in hospital in 1766. He continued to print sermons promoting various charities established to support these new endeavours, alongside local documents such as poll books, lists of voter names and candidates, and ecclesiastical records. His monopoly was, however, short-lived and he was soon in competition with other printers.

5.3 Expanding Networks and Innovating the Press

In 1760, White Jr. moved his premises from the Side to Jevel Groop nearer the river. The volume of ballads that he was printing at this time (forty-five titles can be identified, and the nature of eighteenth-century ephemeral material suggests there would have been more), likely demanded a dedicated press. More space, therefore, would have been needed to

---

[128] Defoe, *Tour*, p. 191. [129] Wesley, *Journal*, p. 248.
[130] Smith, *Sermon Preached*.

house an additional press for other kinds of work.[131] In 1761, he was established enough to take on a partner, Thomas Saint, who had been his journeyman. To counter an increasingly crowded market in Newcastle, White Jr. diversified his business. As well as books, he stocked a wide range of medicines, both retail and wholesale.[132] He also printed medical pamphlets, helping drive this trade to his shop.[133] He was demonstrably interested in new ideas, being the first printer to experiment with the latest innovation: stereotype. For this he collaborated with William Ged, a goldsmith in Edinburgh, to produce *Life of God in the Soul of Man* in 1742. Stereotype was produced using a printing plate, rather than making up a page with loose type, an innovation that sped up the production process considerably.

White Jr.'s canny approach to business is further evident in his dealings with the stamp tax of 1712. His paper, *The Newcastle Courant*, included local news and had a higher number of advertisements in comparison with other similar newspapers.[134] All paper used for printing newspapers had to be purchased from a central office and was stamped at the rate of 1d. per full sheet and ½d. per half sheet. This dramatically increased the production costs of newspapers and affected many publications that were forced to raise the retail price for consumers. By printing one and a half sheets per issue White claimed his publication was a pamphlet, in other words more than four pages long. This meant he only paid tax on each edition, not every copy. By reducing his tax burden he was able to keep costs relatively low for his readers.[135]

As White Jr.'s collaboration with William Ged indicates, the book trade was a cooperative and collaborative business. White's imprint details show the wide circle of people with whom he worked. Initially he continued to work closely with his father, as can be seen by the publication of *The Fall of Tarquin: A Tragedy* in 1713, a work printed by father and son in York and Newcastle.[136] In the same year, one of his sermons was sold by Mr Freeman, a bookseller in Durham. This extended geography indicates a developing

---

[131] I am indebted to Dr Dave Harper of the English and Related Literature department at the University of York for discussion around this point.
[132] Gardner, 'John White', p. 87. [133] Wilson, *Short Remarks*.
[134] Cranfield, *Development*, p. 209. [135] Ibid., p. 18. [136] Hunt, *Fall of Tarquin*.

network in the north-east print trade further afield, though he frequently worked with Newcastle booksellers William Charnley, and James Fleming.[137] Sometimes the extent of distribution was particularly wide. In 1731, White Jr. printed the anonymous *Use of Human Reason*, a tract in defence of the Anglican church, which would subsequently be sold all over the north, including Sunderland, York, Leeds, Hull, Carlisle, and Kendal as well as London.[138]

White Jr.'s network also extended outside the northeast. He worked with booksellers in Cambridge, and he had many contacts in London. The traffic of books and knowledge was two-way; as Barbara Crosbie points out, in addition to producing material that could be classed as 'local' the Newcastle sermons printed by White Jr. often included a London bookseller.[139] His connection to London continued with the increase in the capital's interest in regional news and, from the 1760s, the *Newcastle Courant* became available in London.[140] Nonetheless, his commitment to the North remained. This can be seen in his dealings with the print trade in York, where he collaborated with printers, beginning with his stepmother (Grace White) and nephew (Charles Bourne).

5.4 Return to York and Legacy

In 1716, John White Sr. died. In his will he left 'to my beloved son John' the rents of several houses, plus £100. The printing equipment was left to his wife, Grace, and his grandson, Charles Bourne.[141] Given that White Jr. was already establishing himself in Newcastle and clearly had all the necessary machinery and tools, ready money as well as ongoing income from rents would likely have been more directly beneficial than equipment. The relationship between White Jr. and Grace White and Charles Bourne in York was a productive one. His experience of setting up the *Newcastle Courant* must have been helpful in the establishment of York's first newspaper, the *York Mercury*, which was printed by Grace White from 1719. If the goal of father and son was a family business in York and Newcastle,

---

[137] See Hunt, *Book-trade*. [138] Anon., *Use of Human Reason*.
[139] Crosbie, 'Provincial Purveyors', p. 224. [140] Ibid., p. 218.
[141] Will of John White.

a York newspaper to cover the areas that the *Newcastle Courant* did not would certainly support that ambition. The first issue of the *York Mercury* was 23 February 1719, and the front page shows the extent of distribution northwards to Stockton on Tees, where it met the outer limit of the coverage of the *Newcastle Courant*.

This comfortable collaboration was not to last, however, and by 1724, events outside White Jr.'s control would put at risk his business endeavours in York. Bourne inherited the press fully on Grace White's death in 1721, and six months later married Alice Guy, who had been in John White Sr.'s household for many years. Bourne died in August 1724, and four months later Guy married Thomas Gent, John White Sr.'s previous journeyman. Losing the printing press which had been in his family since 1644 would have been a hard blow for White Jr. According to Gent he tried to prevent the marriage and 'did all that was in his power to keep us asunder'; the subsequent difficult relationship between the two men is documented in Gent's autobiography.[142] The original plans that White Jr. and his father had made for domination of the north-east printing trade looked to be thwarted. However, in 1725 he set up his own York branch on the same street as Gent's press, appointing a manager to oversee the work when he was in Newcastle.[143] In a move that certainly deepened the divide between Gent and White Jr., the first issue of the *York Courant*, a direct competitor to Gent's *York Journal* (the renamed *Mercury*), was produced in August 1725. In 1731, White Jr. was accused of printing seditious material in the *Newcastle Courant* and avoided the risk of persecution in York by changing the name on the *York Courant* to Sarah Coke for a short period.

Though he kept up the York branch of his business for nearly two decades, White Jr. devoted most of his energies to his business in Newcastle. Between 1725 and 1734, when he sold the York branch, White Jr. published eight books in York and thirty-nine in Newcastle. In York, White Jr.'s outputs comprised poetry, songs, and theological

---

[142] Gent, *Life*, p. 148.

[143] Consensus on who was the manager has not been reached. Robert Ward and John Gilfillan are both suggested.

works. During the same period, his Newcastle titles were more varied and included sermons, election printing, and the scientific lectures of Presbyterian Minister John Horsey. He worked with the Hildyards in York, who had been close friends of his father, and with booksellers in London. White Jr.'s standing in York, albeit his secondary professional location, is clear from his election to the position of sheriff of the city in 1734. However, roads between York and Newcastle were notoriously bad and the strain of maintaining two businesses must have been considerable. In the same year as his election to sheriff, he sold his York business to John Gilfillan as a going concern and devoted himself to Newcastle until the end of his career. White Jr. never lost contact with York's print trades, however. His books continued to be sold 'by the booksellers of York', including Francis and John Hildyard and, later, John Hinxman at the Sign of the Bible on Stonegate. In 1762, John Todd took over this shop from Hinxman, and sold White Jr.'s books with his partner Henry Sotheran. There is evidence that White Jr. also recognised the value in keeping professional connections with York for printing opportunities: in 1737, he printed *Roma Meretrix* for Alexander Staples, by then proprietor of the *York Courant*, and in 1760, he reprinted Thomas Gent's chapbook, *The Unhappy Birth, Wicked Life, and Miserable Death of that Vile Traitor, and Apostle, Judas Iscariot*.[144] Gent's chapbook was extremely popular and had already been printed in York, Hull, and Durham; its publication by White Jr. represents a shrewd business decision despite the apparent ongoing antipathy between the two men.[145]

When White Jr. died, his obituary in the *Newcastle Courant* described him as 'candid, affable, charitable and humane'.[146] While these are all positive attributes, they do not reflect his lasting legacy in the printing history of Newcastle. He was the city's first printer, with many others following where he led. The business he established would continue as a going concern for many years after his death. His partner, Thomas Saint, maintained the firm's concentration on popular literature and became well known as a producer of children's books, employing the engraver Thomas

---

[144] Mawer, *Roma Meretrix*. [145] Sessions and Sessions, *Printing in York*, p. 31.
[146] *Newcastle Courant*, 28 January 1769.

Bewick to provide illustrations. Saint passed the business onto his assistant John Hall in 1788, and it was bought by Edward Walker in 1795.[147] White Jr.'s skill in his trade, his energy and commitment, and his entrepreneurial approach to business all combined to put him at the forefront of the creation of a thriving print culture in Newcastle.

---

[147] Hunt, *Book-trade*, pp. 81, 43, 92.

6 Selling the Enlightenment: Mary Cooper and Print Culture (1707–1761) by Lisa Maruca

Mary Cooper has been hiding in plain sight. While she has been called the 'leading' trade publisher of the middle eighteenth century – a fair assessment given that there are more than 2200 ESTC records listing her name in the imprint – she is most frequently only a footnote in eighteenth-century literary and book histories.[148] Even in Michael Treadwell's groundbreaking 'London Trade Publishers, 1675-1750', which introduced this sector of trade to bibliography, she is given only a few sentences – and these (as I discuss below) have conscribed a full understanding of her work.[149] Despite the ubiquity of her name in imprints, the breadth of her partnerships, and a solid reputation as a reliable businesswoman among her contemporaries, there are few scholarly works focusing solely on her.[150] This essay remedies this dearth through a re-evaluation of her work, showing her substantive contribution to print culture across many areas crucial to the Enlightenment project.

6.1 Beyond Political Publishing

Cooper was born in 1707, married Thomas Cooper in 1731, and had four children by 1741. She and Thomas shared a successful print retail business at the Sign of the Globe at 21 Paternoster Row until he died in February 1743. Presumably, like many wives in the print trade, she was familiar with the business and, feasibly, an active partner.[151] The *Daily Advertiser*'s death notice for Thomas pointedly claims that the 'business will be carried on by his widow who has long been conversant in it'.[152] It also attests that he had suffered from a 'long illness' but still left a 'handsome fortune', possibly suggesting the business did not suffer too much during his health crisis. If Mary did have to learn the business after Thomas' death, it did not take

---

[148] Raven, *Business of Books*, p. 172. [149] Treadwell, 'London', pp. 99–134.
[150] Exceptions include Schneller, *Mary Cooper*; Goodman, 'Rogue'.
[151] See Coker, 'Gendered Spheres', pp. 323–36.
[152] Schneller, *Mary Cooper*, p. 20.

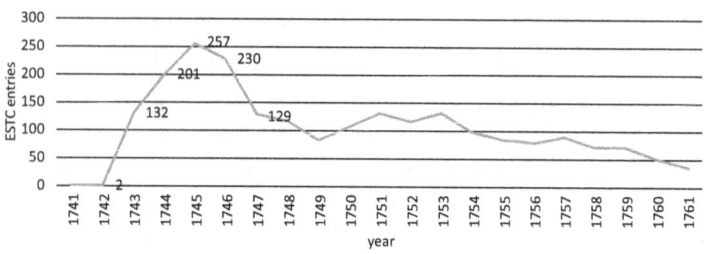

Figure 2 Mary Cooper, ESTC entries per year, 1741–61.

long: 1743 was one of her top years in terms of imprints, and the next three years were even better (see Figure 2). During her three decades in the trade (three times as long as her husband), Mary Cooper's colleagues spoke highly of her. Samuel Richardson, for example, recommended her as someone 'against whom there can be no objection'.[153] John Nichols, the influential editor of *The Gentleman's Magazine*, went further, calling her a 'Publisher of considerable consequence'.[154] When she died in 1761, her estate was administered by her sister, and the business went to her sister's husband, John Hinxman, a York bookseller, who – in a demonstration of the English print trade's small world – had been the apprentice of Mary Cooper's sometime business partner, Robert Dodsley.[155]

Despite the praise of her colleagues, the scant scholarship on Cooper's work perpetuates the idea that her imprint is linked almost exclusively to racy political pamphlets, subterfuge, or even fraud. For example, her entry in H.R. Plomer's influential *Dictionary of the Printers and Booksellers* focuses solely on an anecdote about a 'spurious' book that she 'sold [...] as genuine'.[156] Since then, her work is often used as an example of how misleading mid-eighteenth-century imprints can be.[157] Some descriptions even deploy the language of criminality, claiming, for example, that

---

[153] Treadwell, 'London', p. 134. [154] Nichols, *Anecdotes*, p. 403.
[155] For probate references for both Coopers, see Treadwell, 'London', p. 111, n. 26.
[156] Plomer et al., *Dictionary*, pp. 60–61.
[157] See Feather, 'Business Models', pp. 55–83.

'Cooper was a front whose role was to screen the true producers' and 'provide plausible deniability' or that she was a 'print rogue' in contrast to 'conventional printers and publishers'.[158] References like these depend mostly on understanding her as a trade publisher, the supposed mission of which was to circulate for others anonymous, scandalous, and potentially seditious work. Yet, as Treadwell explains, that was only part of the trade publishers' role, one that, by Cooper's time, was waning.[159] Too much scholarship skips over another important aspect of trade publishing: it connected copyright holders – sometimes not anonymous at all – to someone in the trade with a vast distribution network and a reputation for high sales.[160]

To more accurately assess Cooper's contribution to her trade, then, as well as to the wider culture, we need to understand the full breadth of works she handled. Surveying two representative years of ESTC records with the imprint 'printed for' or 'sold by M. Cooper, at the Globe in Pater-noster-Row' demonstrates the wider scope of what she was selling.[161] The year 1745 was chosen because it is her most prolific year (her name appeared on 257 records), while 1750 is the year in which she owned the copyrights to the highest percentage of the works with her imprint (still only 3% of 108 works).[162] While both are in the prime of her career and only five years apart, the two years differ considerably historically: 1745 was politically tumultuous because of the Jacobite Rising, occurring while the military was away fighting the War of Austrian Succession; 1750 was more peaceful at home and abroad. Analysing the works from these years shows that

---

[158] Box et al., 'Diplomatic Transcription', pp. 224–25; Brant and Rousseau, 'Introduction', p. 6.
[159] Treadwell, 'London', p. 133.
[160] Another misconception is that trade publishers did not own copyrights. In fact, Cooper registered nineteen works, albeit a small percentage of her total output.
[161] Treadwell explains that 'printed for' does not imply financing. Treadwell, 'London', p. 115.
[162] Relying on ESTC data has drawbacks: it is a human-constructed database, with blind spots and errors, and it only records what was deemed worthy of collection and preservation. Nonetheless, it is still useful for noticing overarching trends.

Table 2 ESTC records by topic: 1745 versus 1750.

Topic	1745 number	1745 percent	1750 number	1750 percent
Politics (war, satire, military, world affairs)	120	47%	10	9%
Education, Information, Scholarship	47	18%	45	42%
Religion	34	13%	23	21%
Poetry, arts, literary criticism	27	11%	12	11%
Entertainment (narrative, humour/wit, fiction, drama, gossip)	25	10%	18	17%
Life writing: exemplar and elegy	4	>2%	0	n/a
Total	257		108	

Cooper's inventory went far beyond the political and she was *not* in fact associated only with works that turn over quickly, although that was a part of her business. Table 2, for example, exhibits the topics of her works. While politics was the largest category of work she sold in the turbulent 1745, this comprised less than half her total output for the year. By 1750, this category declined dramatically, replaced by educational and informational works. Table 3 provides information about the length of her works. During both years, works under ten pages constitute a tiny minority of her output, and are often poetry. While we might see this as a problem with ESTC records – short works tend to be ephemeral – it is still clear that most of the works she distributed in 1745 were ten to fifty pages, which would take a bit of time to read and digest, followed by a still substantial number of books longer than fifty pages. By 1750, an even higher majority of her works are in the longest category. Taken together, the range of topics and lengths suggest that Cooper mostly sold works that took time to write and read,

Table 3 ESTC records by length (pages): 1745 versus 1750.

Pages	1745		1750	
	number	percent	number	percent
1–10	26	10%	1	1%
10–50	131	51%	43	40%
51+	100	39%	64	59%

presumably of some complexity. This does not exactly fit the persona of a 'print rogue'.

Moving from percentages to actual works, it is clear that Cooper contributed significantly across several important cultural sectors:

1 Periodicals and the Public Sphere

Part of Cooper's work not captured in my ESTC analysis is her distribution of periodicals, only some of which could be described as political. The twenty periodicals she published 'were fairly evenly divided between *belletristic* miscellanies, essay journals, and theme journals such as *The Modern Husbandman*'.[163] Between 1744 and 1757 alone she was affiliated with 'one daily and five weekly political papers', including *The Daily Gazetteer*, printed by Samuel Richardson (which she and her husband likely owned a share of), and *The Centinel*, which had a run of 104 issues.[164] She worked frequently with Henry Fielding, presumably with her husband when he published *The Champion*, but after his death on *The Jacobite's Journal* and the *True Patriot* (for which her shop was designated to receive post).[165] She also was affiliated with Eliza Haywood's *The Female Spectator*, as well as Robert Dodsley's *The Museum* and *The World*.[166] She thus contributed to the early history of journalism and, in doing so, influenced

---

[163] Schneller, *Mary Cooper*, p. 32.
[164] Schneller, 'Periodical Publishing', pp. 31–33; Schneller, 'John Hill', p. 112.
[165] Harris, 'Literature', p. 102; Baker, 'Henry Fielding', p. 214, n. 5.
[166] Schneller, 'Periodical Publishing', pp. 31–33.

the construction of the public sphere. The Coopers published, for example, a large majority of the heterogeneous works preserved in the Tom's Coffee House Collection.[167] Coffee houses kept materials on hand for members, serving to filter and organise the 'information explosion' of the time.[168] From the city, these discussions rippled out to the rest of the county through distributors like Cooper's network of provincial trade connections.

2 Children's Works and Education

Cooper is perhaps best known for her contributions to quite a different area: the burgeoning sector of children's literature. As Andrea Immel notes, 'of all the new markets for print that emerged between 1695 and 1833, the one for young readers was arguably among the most important to Great Britain's polite, commercial society'.[169] Many standard histories of this field start with John Newbery, but the Coopers first published *A Child's New Play-Thing* in 1742, two years before Newbery's first book. One of its innovations was its target audience of preschool children. It was also the first to include a feature that would later become commonplace, an alphabet printed on a fold-out sheet meant 'to be cut into single Squares for Children to Play with'.[170] After her husband's death, Mary Cooper 'fostered and refined' this text 'through several more editions, and it remained in print for most of the eighteenth century'.[171] She also collaborated with another print widow, Mary Boreman, to produce the two-volume *Christmas-Box for Masters and Missies*, 'the first published example of secular stories for children in England'.[172] Finally, Cooper has been called 'the guiding genius behind the most thrilling of all the experimental books of the 1740s, if not the most thrilling of all English children's books *tout court*', *Tommy Thumb's Pretty Song Book* (1744).[173] This was the first collection of nursery rhymes known in print – except that it was actually all *engraved*, a time-consuming but economically advantageous method allowing for the delight of a picture on every page.[174] This was commercially successful, a 'virtual overnight

---

[167] Ellis, 'Coffee-House Libraries', pp. 25–28. [168] Ibid., pp. 35–39.
[169] Immel, 'Children's Books', p. 736. [170] Anon., *Child's New*, n.p.
[171] Alderson, 'New Playthings', p. 191. [172] Ibid., p. 193. [173] Ibid.
[174] Immel and Alderson, 'Nurse Lovechild', p. 23.

publishing phenomenon'.[175] Imitators and plagiarists abounded and Tom Thumb 'branded' work, including Cooper's own, appeared through the 1770s.[176] With its preface featuring an 'English Lady' giving the parenting advice of 'Nurse Lovechild', it also paved the way for the professionalization of women in educational print. During her career, Mary Cooper continued to be someone 'reliably hospitable to the production of children's books', as well as scores of other educational and instructional works for children as well as adults.[177]

3 Literary Works

Mary Cooper was also involved in retailing several now canonical authors. This category is small numerically, but its cultural legacy is large. She and her husband sold multiple editions of the octavo *Works of Alexander Pope, Esq.* from 1737 to 1743, as well as several versions of his *Imitations of Horace*. By herself she published a quarto version of the *Dunciad* printed by William Bowyer, the first book she registered with the Stationers' Company.[178] She also registered two of Edward Young's *Complaint; or Night Thoughts* (the seventh and eighth nights), although she is named on the imprint as selling seventeen of them. With Robert Dodsley as publisher, sometimes anonymously, she sold Jonathan Swift's *Three Sermons* (1744); Lady Mary Wortley Montagu's *Six Town Eclogues*; Samuel Johnson's *Irene* (1749) and 'The Vanity of Human Wishes' (1749); Thomas Gray's 'Elegy Written in a Country Churchyard' (1751); and many other poets admired then and barely remembered now, including some of Dodsley's own authored works. David Hume's *Philosophical Essays Concerning Human Understanding* (1751) appeared under her imprint, and she retailed the first volume of Lawrence Sterne's *Tristram Shandy* (1760). She also sold older works, such as translations of Greek and Roman classics, and – then considered the opposite end of the spectrum – was involved in several new editions of *Robinson Crusoe*. Indeed, she was one of the top distributors of the still newish novel, although only thirty-five imprints have been traced,

---

[175] Ibid., pp. 2, 15. [176] Ibid., pp. 40–41. [177] Ibid., pp. 13–14.
[178] Pope, *Dunciad*. For more Register details, see my Data Appendix, https://bit.ly/MCData.

a small fraction of her total.[179] Francis Coventry's *The History of Pompey the Little: Or, The Life and Adventures of a Lap-Dog* (three editions from 1751 to 1752) was one of her more popular offerings.

To understand Mary Cooper as a woman who sold and distributed all these plus more than 2,000 other works is to recognise her importance not just to the print trade but the culture writ large. The Globe must have been a site where people went to fill a variety of reading needs. Her shop would have been known as the place to go, not just to debate politics or the latest military incursion but to delight in the latest poetry and arts essays, to help educate and amuse one's children, to foster religious contemplation, or to discover the latest in science. Given this depth and breadth of output, we need to recognise and appreciate the role Mary Cooper played in the construction of the literate, engaged, informed, and entertained citizen of the eighteenth century.

---

[179] Orr, 'Tactics', p. 405; Raven, 'Britain, 1750–1830', p. 434.

7 The 'Indefatigable' Ann Ward, Printer in York (1715/6–1789) by Kaley Kramer

Despite being the proprietor of one of York's largest and most significant printing houses for nearly thirty years, Ann Ward presents a challenge for scholarship: she left few traces of her own life and few records beyond the outputs of her press. Where she appears, it is frequently connected to two key publications: the first printing of Laurence Sterne's *The Life and Opinions of Tristram Shandy, Gentleman* (vols 1&2, 1759/1760), and the *York Courant*, the newspaper she inherited from her husband, Cesar Ward, in April 1759, and directed until her death in 1789. As a woman with a long and successful career in the regional print trade, Ward offers an illustrative case study both of women in the eighteenth-century regional print trades and the self-fashioning of regional cities through print. Feminist book history and print history scholarship has already opened avenues into recovering occluded histories, including women's work in overseeing presses, participating in the material labour of creating books, and in the selection, support, and management of inventory. This chapter joins such crucial recovery work through what Valerie Wayne calls 'responsible speculation', arguing that the material and commercial evidence of her press amply demonstrates Ward's agency within the eighteenth-century York business of print.[180]

7.1 Ann Ward and the Mid-Century York Print Trades

Ann (née Hays or Hayes, 1715/16) likely met Cesar Ward in Scarborough, where he had a bookshop with Richard Chandler; they married in 1738. Ann joined Cesar in York and their first child was registered at St Michael's parish in the same year. While Ward and Chandler were initially extremely successful partners, by the early 1740s their business was experiencing considerable difficulty. After an elaborate publishing venture resulted in debt, Chandler committed suicide in 1744 and Ward declared bankruptcy in

---

[180] Wayne, *Women's Labour*, p. 19.

1745.[181] His reputation in York was solid enough, however, that friends and supporters enabled him to re-establish his press and eventually continue the editorship of the *Courant*.[182] After a brief illness, Cesar died in late April 1759, leaving Ann solely responsible for both the business and their large family.[183] The *Courant* continued uninterrupted with Ann Ward the sole name on the paper (as 'A.Ward') from 1 May 1759 until 1 April 1788, when her son-in-law, George Peacock, formally joined the business.

When Ward took over her husband's press in Leopard Lane, across from St Martin's Church on Coney Street, York's population was well-served by a lively and (at times) competitive print market, including printers Thomas Gent, Nick Nicholson, and John Jackson, Jr. Connections between the York print trades and other regional centres such as Newcastle and London were well established: John White, Jr., son of John White of York (d.1715), ran successful businesses in both York and Newcastle and established the *York Courant* in 1725 (see Chapter 5); John Hinxman, proprietor of the Sign of the Bible in Stonegate, had apprenticed with the great London printer Robert Dodsley. Ward's press was thus part of a vibrant local print trade, satisfying demands from professional, ecclesiastical, and popular readerships. Throughout her career, Ward published sermons, catalogues, poetry, novels, and plays, as well as various ephemeral and more salacious materials, such as an early report of the trial of Eugene Aram for murder, John Hawkridge's medical treatises, directions for repairing roads, and guidebooks to the local area.[184] L.P. Curtis, while lauding her as 'indefatigable', disparagingly summarises Ward's career – outside of *Tristram Shandy* – as one of merely

---

[181] See Sessions and Sessions, *Printing in York*, p. 37 and Ferdinand, 'Cesar Ward'.

[182] Sessions and Sessions, *Printing in York*, p. 37.

[183] Of their twelve children, eight were living when Cesar died. I am grateful to Sarah Griffin at York Minster Library and Archive for research into the scant traces of Ann's life.

[184] The novel was [Francis Gentleman], *A Trip to the Moon* (1764); poetry by William Mason and Thomas Gray; Hitchcock's play, *The Macaroni* (1773); seed catalogues and book lists for local trades; Anon, 'Genuine Account' (1759); Hawkridge, *Treatise* (1764); 'Directions for Repairing Roads' (broadsheet, 1765); *An Accurate Depiction & History of the York Minster* and *Nomina Villarum Eboracensium* (both 1768).

'printing the dreary manuscripts which came to her' and crediting her skill as 'irreproachable' only compared with the 'dullness' of the material she printed.[185]

Ward herself had a higher estimation of her skills, publicly reassuring the readership of the *Courant* in the first issue after Cesar Ward's death that the paper would 'be carried on with the same Diligence and Impartiality as before; under the Conduct of the same Person, who, for some Years last past, has had the principal Management of it'.[186] Signing her name to this brief note, Ward provides a reassuring continuity for her readership and subtly asserts her own labour and capability to run the press. Under her ownership, the press moved to new and larger premises facing the river on Coney Street, previously occupied by Kidd's Coffee-House. Robert Davies offers a tantalising glimpse of the public interest in spaces of print, noting that 'in January 1774 Miss Marshall gave a concert in [the printing room]'.[187] These more public, accessible, and central offices indicate Ann Ward's confidence as a business owner and as a valued member of York society.

Ward's first major publishing venture was Laurence Sterne's *Tristram Shandy* in late autumn of 1759. Cesar Ward had printed Sterne's earlier works, including sermons and his controversial pamphlet, *A Political Romance* (1759); he was also a member of the Good Humour Club, a convivial society established in York in 1724, which included Sterne as well as the bookseller John Hinxman.[188] Cesar, however, died on 24 April 1759 and the earliest evidence for Sterne's plans for the book is from June 1759 when he wrote to Robert Dodsley.[189] Given Sterne's familiarity with Ward's press, he likely knew Ann's skills as a printer. His letter to Dodsley indicates his confidence in the printing house he has in mind: Dodsley's press was, by the 1750s, one of the most important in London and Sterne assures him that *Shandy* will be printed in York 'in so creditable a way as to paper, type, &c., as to do no dishonour to you, who,

---

[185] Curtis, 'The First Printer', p. 781. [186] *York Courant*, 1 May 1759.
[187] Davies, *Memoir*, p. 261, note.
[188] Curtis, 'The First Printer', 778. See Williams, 'Good Humour Club', pp. 144–45.
[189] Curtis, 'The First Printer', p. 778.

I know, never chuse to print a book meanly'.[190] Ward herself continued to work with James Dodsley long after Sterne – and *Shandy* – left York for London. *Shandy* may be the most illustrious product of Ward's press, but for her business it primarily served as a gateway to future opportunities in London.[191]

Ward retained David Russell, who had worked at the press under Cesar Ward, granting him shares in the business. Russell is often mentioned in relation to Ann Ward's press but there is no consensus on his role and assessments vary considerably: Davies calls Russell an 'able compositor' and 'superintendent of the press'; the Sessions go so far as to consider him a 'co-printer' with Ward of *Tristram Shandy*.[192] Hannah Barker's work on political perspectives in York newspapers during the mid to late eighteenth century Reform Movement, for which York was an important centre, indicates that Russell was an important contact for the *Courant*.[193] Given the scope and size of Ward's press, it is reasonable that Russell was the contact for some contributors and customers. As Valerie Wayne, Helen Smith, Paula McDowell, and Lisa Maruca have noted, print businesses were necessarily communal to varying extents: the complexity of the machinery, the material requirements of print, and the multiple demands of regulators, customers, stakeholders, and clients required multiple personnel, most of whom were forgotten or obscured by the focus on single, named owners of a given printing house.[194] Russell worked under Cesar Ward as well, but it

---

[190] Sterne, *Letters*, p. 81.

[191] Mason, *Scarborough*; Mason, *The Poems of Mr Gray*. See also Evelyn, *Silva* and Evelyn, *Terra*.

[192] Davies, *Memoir*, p. 261; Sessions and Sessions, *Printing in York*, p. 38. Barker calls Russell the 'day-to-day' manager of the *Courant*, referencing Ian R. Christie's *Wilkes, Wyvill, and Reform* (*Newspapers*, p. 157); Christie, however, refers to Russell as the 'assistant publisher' (p. 194, fn. 2). Ferdinand notes that she was '*assisted* by the *printer*, David Russell' ('Ann Ward', my emphasis); Gardner calls him Ward's 'manager' and 'the paper's conductor' (*Business*, pp. 87, 204).

[193] Barker, *Newspapers*, pp. 149, 156.

[194] See Wayne, *Women's Labour*; Smith, *'Grossly Material Things'*; McDowell, *Grub Street*; Maruca, *The Work of Print*.

is his role after Ann Ward took control that receives so much speculation, illustrating the ways women's labour has been undervalued.

Ward was, however, always the sole name and voice of the press. In addition to the notice immediately after Cesar's death, Ward spoke for the business and to her readership to keep them informed about changes as needed; for example, on 25 June 1770, she wrote a substantial notice in the second column of the first page of a price increase per issue from two-and-a-halfpence to threepence (or '13s. per year'). She writes a concise but thorough history of the Duty charged on newspapers, framing the relatively low price increase as an 'Instance of Gratitude for the Favours of the Public' while noting that the increased duty meant 'several hundred Pounds must be employed in carrying on the Business, more than before'.[195] Ward positions herself as the sole authority at the *Courant* and reminds her readers of her role in the business, closing the item by identifying herself as the 'Printer' and offering her 'respectful Thanks' to the patrons, acknowledging 'the great Obligations which, nor for a long Course of Years, she has ow'd to the Favour of the Public'.[196]

7.2 Regional News and A. Ward's York Courant, 1759–1789

The *Courant* was the mainstay of Ward's press: it appeared weekly on Tuesdays and had a distribution network that extended to London. By 1772, the layout increased from three to four columns on each page, with some variation where needed for exceptional items. News from London, including international reports, received by post from individuals or gleaned from other newspapers, took the top place, starting with 'Friday's Post' in the first column of page one, followed by more recent news (Saturday, Sunday, or Monday) in that column and the next and then carried over to the first column of page two. York and local regional news began on page two; page three frequently carried shipping news; and pages three and four were also often taken up with advertisements, racing news, and horses for 'cover' (breeding). Organising news by date of receipt, rather than through

---

[195] *York Courant*, no. 2648, 25 June 1770. In this item, Ward refers to herself as the 'Printer'.

[196] *York Courant*, no. 2648, 25 June 1770.

thematic sections, preserved an epistolary style, with the editor standing in for the letter-writer. The *Courant* created a familiar conversation between interested and mutually engaged parties, rather than adopting the disinterested pose of 'reportage'.

Advertisements and 'items' in the paper indicate a wide regional readership, with notices for sales, positions, business opportunities, and services from Lincolnshire, across Yorkshire, and into Lancashire and Northumberland. The *Courant* had a much smaller circulation when it began in 1725 under White, Jr., who sold it from his own shop 'nigh St. Helen's Church in Stonegate' and through a 'Mr. Ryles' in Hull and Beverley.[197] By 1760, after Ann Ward took over, it was available across Yorkshire and into Lancashire and the Midlands as well as at coffeehouses in Fleet Street, Paternoster Row, and the Royal Exchange, and 'Mr. Bristow's, Bookseller and Lottery-Office Keeper, at the West-End of St. Paul's, London'.[198] London connections were kept prominently at the top of the paper, indicating an effort to bridge the distance between York and the capital, lending authority to the reports Ward selected for her York readership.

While the *Courant* emphasised its London network, it was first and foremost a regional paper: national and international topics were a key feature but it had to balance these potentially controversial perspectives with coverage of local news. The *Courant* was Tory under Cesar Ward; under Ann Ward, during the 1770s and 1780s, however, the paper was involved in the national reform movement, largely due to the influence of Christopher Wyvill.[199] From 1769 onwards, ongoing letters, queries, and responses to and about 'Freeholders' of Yorkshire were frequent, as well as items connecting the Yorkshire Association with other regions such as Durham and reformist pieces from further afield, such as an extract from the *Public Register, or, Freeman's Journal* in Dublin by 'A hater of Priestcraft'.[200] Through editorial decisions, including accepting paid pieces as well as selecting which London papers were represented, the *Courant*

---

[197] *York Courant*, no. 202, 22 July 1729.
[198] *York Courant*, no. 1785, 2 January 1760. [199] Barker, *Newspapers*, p. 139.
[200] *York Courant*, no. 2334, 10 July 1770.

could also rally audiences for a particular cause or political position, particularly where these affected the local population.

A genteel and cultured city emerges throughout Ward's tenure at the *Courant*, which reflects an audience interested in sociability and a civic self-fashioning evident in publicising certain kinds of activities (philanthropy, upper-class sports, cultural events). On the other hand, items about land use, crops and husbandry, ensure that such sociability is grounded in key local economies. The *Courant* also shaped perceptions of York through advertisements and notices. In 1764, for example, advertisements included various genteel trades in the city, such as silversmiths, jewellers, and linen drapers, as well as notices about inoculations.[201] These products suggest a fashionable and affluent citizenry interested in the latest aesthetic trends and medical advances. In August 1769, the paper carried a list of subscribers to the York Assembly Rooms; in 1784, notices about game laws and fishing rights on manor lands were more numerous in the pages, which also included lists of hemp and flax growers in the area.[202] By 1772, the paper's extensive regional distribution appears, for example, in marriage and death notices from Manchester and Lancaster.[203] While York was removed, geographically, from the capital, the *Courant* indicates an avid interest in international events, whether that was 'plantation news' from South Carolina, regular updates of ships landing and unloading imported commodities at Hull, or revolutions overseas – as a 'notice to the inhabitant householders of the Borough of Pontefract' from 'C[harles].J[ames]. Fox' suggests.[204]

Ward enjoyed a long and stable ownership of the press, outlasting several rival York papers while continuing to produce respected and admired books and official publications. The wide-ranging appeal of the *Courant*, evident in its distribution and readership, was due to her finely tuned understanding of local interests, which included national and

---

[201] *York Courant*, no. 1997, 7 February 1764; no. 2287, 29 August 1769.
[202] *York Courant*, no. 2287, 29 August 1769.
[203] *York Courant*, no. 2581, 14 March 1775.
[204] *York Courant*, no. 2581, 14 March 1775. Charles James Fox was a radical Whig, antagonist of George III, and staunch supporter of the American Revolution.

international issues and events. Her skills as a printer and her business acumen in establishing productive partnerships as far as London and Edinburgh ensured that her press grew throughout her tenure. The last issue of the *Courant* that appeared with her name was 7 April 1789; she died on Friday 10 April. The *Courant* printed a brief notice, identifying her as, 'for many Years, the Printer of this Paper' and a woman of 'universal Esteem'.[205] Ward left the press to her son-in-law, George Peacock, and it was later directed by her grandson, Cesar Peacock (1809–1819), and her granddaughter, Ann Peacock (1819). While her own understanding of her role in York's print-trades remains elusive, the records of her press and her professional life offer a remarkable portrait of women's involvement in every aspect of a thriving and successful press.

---

[205] *York Courant*, no. 3217, 14 April 1789.

8 Anne Fisher (1719–1778): Not Simply a Printer's Wife by Barbara Crosbie

Anne Fisher (1719–1778) began her working life as a schoolteacher and author of educational books before going on to run a successful printing business in Newcastle upon Tyne alongside her husband, Thomas Slack.[206] She has, with some justification, been described as the 'first female grammarian'.[207] But outside of the field of linguistics her achievements have gained relatively little attention, and her contribution to the print trade has tended to be reduced to that of an able assistant in what is generally assumed to have been her husband's printing office and bookshop.

Fisher's lack of recognition is indicative of a general obfuscation of female contributions to the print trade. This is in large part because married women's labour is obscured by their legal status. In theory, if not always in practice, the laws of coverture prevented wives from owning property and entering into a contract in their own name. As a consequence, women who died before their spouse, as Fisher did, often left little direct evidence of their working lives, which helps to explain why most of the women who have been acknowledged as proprietors of printing businesses were widows. Compounding this is the interpretative bias that results from the assumption, however true, that the print trade was dominated by men. For instance, unnamed staff in a printing office are assumed to have been men unless proven otherwise, while the probable work of wives and daughters has too often been overlooked. The case of Fisher's daughter, Sarah Slack, offers a useful example of this. Sarah was bequeathed the print shop when Fisher's husband, Thomas Slack, died in 1784, but it was only on marrying the printer Solomon Hodgson a year later that the executors of her father's will released her assets, handing them over to her new husband. Technically, then, the print business was transferred between

---

[206] This chapter draws on Crosbie, *Age Relations*, pp. 52–87; and Crosbie, 'Anne Fisher and the Union Street Press'. Fisher's first name is variously spelled with and without an 'e'. I have chosen to use the formal version of her name as it appeared in her advertisements and her baptism records rather than the familiar spelling used in her letters.

[207] Rodríguez-Gil, 'Ann Fisher', n.p.

two men, and Sarah is not credited with being a printer until after her husband died in 1800. Yet she had grown up in a printing family with a mother who was an active partner in the family firm; she had inherited this printing business before she was married, and she proved herself more than capable of running the business successfully in widowhood. There is a growing recognition that it is implausible to conclude such women were ignorant of their trade while wives, and the onus of proof should not require their names to appear on imprints before their contribution is assumed.[208] It is in this context that the evidence of Fisher's role in the print trade is so important, as she provides insights into the working life of a printer's wife.

8.1 Anne Fisher's New Grammar

Fisher was born in 1719 in the hamlet of Old Scale, not far from Lorton in Cumberland, and her father, Henry Fisher, was a yeoman farmer. It is not clear when she relocated to Newcastle upon Tyne, but she had evidently made the move across the Pennines by 1745. This is when her first and most successful publication, *A New Grammar*, appeared in print. This book, which was regularly reprinted in both Newcastle and London, ran to more than thirty editions, and only three English grammars published during the eighteenth century spawned more. *A New Grammar* was a significant intervention in the highly contentious debates over English grammar at this time. It was pirated and plagiarised, and Fisher's ideas were widely copied. Grammar was a very male genre and for a woman to devise a new grammar was, without question, breaching the boundaries of gender expectations. A desire to conceal her gender from her publishers and the public might therefore explain why some of the earliest editions of Anne Fisher's grammar were credited to 'D[aniel] Fisher and others', and even when she was acknowledged as the sole author she used the gender neutral A. Fisher, the pen name she adopted throughout her career.

Within months of *A New Grammar* first appearing in print, Fisher opened a girls' school in Newcastle where she taught grammar alongside needlework. Again, this was breaching gender expectations. Grammar was

---

[208] There are several examples in Stenner et al., *People of Print*; see especially, Woodring (2023), 'Ruth Raworth', p. 46.

traditionally a subject taught to wealthier boys by a learned grammar master as part of a Classical education. The mid-century vernacular grammars (Fisher's being one of the first) were said to be more practical, rewarding, and even (according to Fisher) enjoyable for the scholar of English. In her preface Fisher claimed 'any person of a tolerable capacity may, in a short time, be learned to write English independent of the knowledge of any other tongue, and that as properly and correctly as if for the press'.[209] Her use of 'learned' as opposed to 'taught' was not the only example of northern speech patterns in her grammar but more significant here is the link she made between education and printing. Printers had a vested interest in improving literacy rates, and not just amongst would-be authors. As the book publisher James Lackington noted a generation later, since children had been 'pleased and entertained as well as instructed' they were learning to read at an earlier age, and this developed a 'relish for books in many [that would] last as long as life'.[210] In this respect, Fisher's influence in classrooms across the region and beyond, from girls' boarding schools, to boys' grammar schools, and more elementary mixed-sex writing schools, helped to create the increasingly literate customer base upon which the print trade depended.

In 1751, at the age of thirty-two, Fisher married the printer Thomas Slack, who was at that time employed by Isaac Thompson, the Newcastle publisher of *A New Grammar*. It is therefore likely that her husband-to-be had printed several editions of her book, and this may even be how they met. Either way, this was evidently a marriage made in print and it marked the beginning of a very successful partnership. It also marked the beginning of Fisher's reproductive labour, and she spent much of the next seventeen years pregnant, giving birth every one to three years, with the last of her nine daughters born in 1768, when she was forty-eight. There is no evidence to suggest she continued her school after she became Mrs Slack, but writing was something that could be done around her domestic commitments, and she continued to publish educational books that often appeared in print for the first time during breaks between childbirths: *A New Grammar* (1745), retitled in 1762 as *A Practical New Grammar*, had its twenty-eighth official

---

[209] Fisher, *A New Grammar*, p. v.
[210] Lackington, *Memoirs*, p. 391; cited in Pickering, *John Locke*, pp. 390–91.

edition published in 1795, and possibly pirated 'new editions' thereafter; *The Pleasing Instructor: or, Entertaining Moralist* (1756) saw its seventh edition published in 1770, before pirated and copycat books flooded the market; *The New English Tutor: or, Modern Preceptor* (1762) also ran to at least seven editions; *A New English Exercise Book* (1770) had possibly only one edition; and *An Accurate New Spelling Dictionary, and Expositor of the English Language* (1773 second edition) appeared in at least six editions.

8.2 Anne Fisher Entrepreneur

When the Slacks married, Fisher's entrepreneurial skills were seemingly greater than her husband's, and in the years to come she was evidently a driving force in their print business. In this context it is noteworthy that Thomas Slack was still employed by Isaac Thompson when the first publications 'printed for T. Slack' were produced and, significantly, most of this early output was authored by Fisher. Taking control of the Newcastle print runs of Fisher's books (which often appeared in simultaneous London imprints) allowed the Slacks to maximise their profits from her authorship. Consequently, when they opened their print office and shop, known as the Printing Press, in 1763, her success as an author must have contributed significantly to their working capital.

The Printing Press was situated in the bustling centre of town, an area at the foot of the Bigg Market, variously described as the head of Middle Street or Union Street. Newcastle was, at this time, one of the largest print centres outside of London and so this was not a question of filling a gap in the market; instead, the Slacks had to carve out a niche in a highly competitive environment. This they did to great effect. Their shop became known as a cultural venue where artists, authors, poets, and local luminaries would meet to discuss the issues of the day. The Printing Press has been presented as Thomas Slack's venture, and even when Fisher's involvement is acknowledged, her contribution has often been diminished by the assumption it was 'her husband's business'; in the words of Peter Isaac, Thomas was 'ably assisted by his wife' in his shop, but it was, nonetheless, *his* shop.[211]

---

[211] See Isaac, 'Fisher, Anne (1719–1778)'; also Isaac, 'Thomas Slack, 1723?– 1784', p. 19.

Even if Fisher's only role in the business had been presiding over the literary sociability of the Printing Press, this should not be seen as a trivial adjunct to the real business done by men. Establishing their shop as a cultural hub was integral to their trade and the overall success of the business. But Fisher's position in Slack and Co. was not, in any case, limited to keeping shop. Letters she wrote to the poet John Cunningham demonstrate that she undertook a range of activities, from making deals to organising sales, and using her contacts to promote publications, including an association with the bluestocking Elizabeth Montagu, who spent part of each year living just outside of Newcastle. These letters also reveal that Fisher was involved in, and understood, the various stages of the book production process, and that she took on the day-to-day management of the Printing Press when her husband was out of town.[212] Looking back some half a century after the last of Fisher's children died, *The Monthly Chronicle* (1890) was unequivocal about her position in the Printing Press; while describing it as a joint venture ran by both Mr and Mrs Slack, it was said 'the couple were not merely printers and booksellers, but bookmakers and journalists as well'.[213]

Perhaps the most telling evidence of this collaborative partnership is found in the *Newcastle Chronicle*, the newspaper the Slacks established in 1764. This publication was central to the success of their business. It not only provided a regular income from newspaper sales and advertising revenue but was also a vehicle for promoting both their products and the literary culture upon which their sales depended. Like the Printing Press, it is generally assumed that this was Thomas Slack's venture. Even when it is conceded that Mr and Mrs Slack 'probably co-operated on the newspaper', Thomas is described as the 'founder and printer' of the *Chronicle*.[214] Nevertheless, Fisher's input was evident from the outset. In fact, one of the things that set this publication apart from its rivals was that it specifically targeted female readers, and a promotional flyer assured 'the Ladies' that the paper would not just report political

---

[212] See Hodgson, 'John Cunningham', pp. 83–100; Williams, 'Printing', pp. 93–116.
[213] Scott, *Monthly Chronicle*, p. 224. [214] Welford, 'Early Newcastle', p. 37.

and business news but would also contain polite literature alongside subjects tending to 'their edification and amusement'.[215] The Slacks were evidently working together to maximise their potential readership. What is more, Fisher had just produced the first edition of *The Ladies' Own Memorandum-Book* (published annually from 1764 to 1805), and there was a clear parallel in its content and the aspects of the *Chronicle* aimed at 'the Ladies'. So here we see a dovetailing of entrepreneurial activity reminiscent of the early stages of her career when she published a grammar that she used in her school. The *Chronicle* was Whig-leaning, but it was not London-centric like the other Whig newspaper in town, the *Newcastle Journal*. The Slacks' provincial self-confidence made theirs a radical paper in the political environment of the 1760s. But so did Fisher's particular touch; after all, newspapers were, like grammar, something conventionally assumed to be produced by men for a male readership.

8.3 Conclusion: Not Divorced from the Trade

Fisher's gender was an asset to Slack and Co. She was successful as a woman, not despite being one. Marriage did not limit her opportunities, but motherhood did inevitably shape her working life, and her hands-on contribution in the business must have had an inverse correlation with her levels of reproductive labour. For instance, when the Printing Press first opened in 1763 the Slacks had six daughters aged one, three, five, eight, nine, and ten, and there was another baby to care for by the time the *Newcastle Chronicle* first appeared in print. This inevitably limited the amount of time she could spend in the printing office and shop, no matter how much domestic support she had. But the responsibilities of motherhood did not undermine her intellectual, entrepreneurial, and financial input to Slack and Co., and she evidently understood the book trade from composition, through production, to marketing and sales. And yet Fisher's obituary in the newspaper she had helped to establish described her as 'Mrs Slack wife of Mr Slack, printer' before going on to say 'her character thro' life, in her family as well as social connections, is so well known, as need not to be

---

[215] Slack and Co., 'Just Published', p. 1.

enlarged upon here'.[216] So even in death, and despite this assumed notability, there was no public acknowledgement of her publications let alone her involvement in the print trade. Maybe to an eighteenth-century eye there was little need to point out the obvious: that printers' wives were not divorced from the trade. Nonetheless, convention conspired with the laws of coverture to hide her achievements from the historical record.

[216] *Newcastle Chronicle*, 2 May 1778.

9 Sold at the Vestry: John Rippon (1751–1836) and the Hymnbook Trade by Dominic Bridge

John Rippon was an astute entrepreneur who used innovative commercial practices to develop a monopoly over the Baptist hymnbook trade during his career. Under his pastorship, Carter Lane in Southwark, London, became the largest Baptist Church in the country, attracting over a thousand members. Rippon is well known for his active role in Baptist life on both sides of the Atlantic and is particularly remembered for his contributions to Baptist hymnody. His *Selection of Hymns* (first published in 1787) was built on Isaac Watts' collection and ran into twenty-seven editions during his lifetime. His reputation as a minister and hymnologist has disguised the substantial publishing practices that accompanied his involvement in the international Baptist community. In part due to his hymnbook sales, Rippon died with an estimated wealth of £100,000, far beyond the stipend of a Baptist minister.[217] Rippon's financial success can be attributed to his much broader and previously unnoticed book trade practices and the commercial nous through which he built a substantial publishing and bookselling business from the vestry of his meeting house.

9.1 Baptist Annual Register

Rippon kept up correspondence with Baptist churches in England, Wales, and America, collecting data on congregation business and church leadership. He collated and published this information in his *Baptist Annual Register* (1793–1802), which could be bought in London, Bristol, Edinburgh, Dublin, New York, Philadelphia, Boston, Baltimore, Richmond, Savanah, and Charleston. The *Register* listed 'the principal books and pamphlets which have been lately printed by the Baptists; including a few other publications of respectable persons, who are described by the denominations to which they belong'.[218] Despite the self-proclaimed denominational objectives of the edition, Rippon exploited his editorial role of the *Register* to support his commercial publishing

---

[217] Manley, 'Rippon, John'. [218] Rippon, *Baptist Annual Register*.

practices. The register contained three lists of publications for the years 1790, 1791, and 1792. Not all of the listed books were sold by Rippon, but his personal bookselling and publishing interests took increasing precedence over others.

The *Register* itself was published by Rippon. Although it was not unusual for individuals in the eighteenth century to publish specialist works independently of larger publishing houses, this edition was part of Rippon's much larger publishing and bookselling output. Rippon's vestry appears frequently as an imprint in a variety of works, including those promoted by the register, his own published writings, editions to which he contributed, books from other authors, and his hymnbook collections. The imprint appears in a number of variations, including 'Sold at Dr. Rippon's Vestry, Tooley Street', 'May be had at the vestry of Dr. Rippon's meeting-house, in Carter Lane, Tooley Street', 'by the pewopeners at the vestry of Mr. Rippon's meeting-house in Carter Lane, Southwark', and, simply, 'May be had of the author'.[219]

Of the fifty works promoted in the 1790 list 'of the principal books and pamphlets which have been lately printed by the Baptists', eleven were available from Rippon's vestry, three of which were his own publications. The first three works advertised are by Rev. Isaac Backus. These works do not contain any prefatory or editorial contributions by Rippon and his imprint does not appear on their title pages but readers are still advised to 'Apply for the above to Mr. John Rippon, or to the Rev. Mr. Timothy Thomas, London', should they wish to purchase a copy.[220] This indicates that Rippon presented the vestry to his large international audience as a *de facto* bookseller's shop that stocked the works of other publishers and authors.

For the following editions, Rippon provided more explanatory gloss which took up far more space in the list than works not sold at the vestry. One example is Rev. Mr. Jedidiah Morse's *The American Geography; or, A View of the Present Situation of the United States of America*, which receives a detailed summary of its contents and is advertised as 'Illustrated with two

---

[219] Rippon and Walker, *Selection of Tunes*; Rippon, *Selection of Psalm*; Rippon, *Andrew Gifford*; Rippon, *Discourse*.

[220] Backus, *A History*.

Sheet Maps – one of the Southern, the other of the Northern States, neatly and elegantly engraved, and more correct than any that have hitherto been published'.[221] Rippon then included three of his own publications in the register: *A Confession of the Faith; A Sermon Occasioned by the Death of Rev. Andrew Gifford;* and *A Sermon at the execution of Moses Paul*.[222] The edition of *A Sermon Occasioned by the Death of Rev. Andrew Gifford* (1784) uses the imprint 'by the pewopeners at the vestry of Mr Rippon's meeting house in Carter Lane, Southwark',[223] suggesting that the employees of the church were working for Rippon's bookselling business as well as the church itself. Below these literary publications is an advert that briefly mentions his hymn collection:

> These three articles, and also his Selection of Hymns from the best authors, intended to be an appendix to Dr. Watts' Psalms and Hymns, may be had of Mr. Rippon, and at No. 7, Carter-lane, Tooley street, near London Bridge; also of Silly and Robinson, London; Brown at Bristol, and Binns at Leeds.

While Rippon used the register to promote works written and published by a range of authors and publishers, he only included psalm and hymnbooks published by himself. This was not routine behaviour. An equivalent publication by Church of England rector William Vincent recommended several editions to his readers in his *Considerations on Parochial Music* (1790).[224] Vincent was not financially invested in hymnbook production or sales so could recommend multiple editions without damaging his publishing interests.[225] However, he did use his authority as a Church of England rector to warn his readers that with 'Hymns and all compositions not authorised by the Church, great caution is required'.[226] Vincent's publication provided spiritual instruction, guiding readers in their choice

---

[221] Rippon, *Baptist Annual Register*, p. 123.
[222] The last of which is also offered in Welsh translation.
[223] Rippon, *Andrew Gifford*. [224] See Vincent, *Considerations*, p. 36.
[225] See Trowles, 'Vincent, William'. [226] Vincent, *Considerations*, p. 37.

of hymnbooks and encouraging them to develop the skills to discern for themselves the appropriate musical works to use in church.

Rippon, on the other hand, took full advantage of the promotional opportunities that arose from his editorial control of the *Register* to build a monopoly over psalm and hymnbook production for Baptist Churches in Great Britain and the United States by ignoring competitors. Several Baptists wrote and published hymns in the first half of the eighteenth century, including David Cully (1726), Anne Dutton (1734), Daniel Turner (1747), Benjamin Wallin (1750), and Edward Trivett (1755).[227] There was no shortage of direct competitors to Rippon's hymnbooks, including Anne Steele's *Poems on Subjects Chiefly Devotional* (1760), Samuel Deacon's *A New Composition of Hymns and Poems* (1785, 1797), *Hymns and Spiritual Songs* (1793), and John Deacon's *A New and Large Collection of Hymn and Psalms* (1800).[228] But despite the variety of editions on the market Rippon managed to position, his own publications as the only option available to readers of the *Register*.

Rippon became increasingly monopolistic in his use of the lists. The list for 1791 does not contain any literary works that were published by Rippon or sold at the vestry. This is because most of Rippon's works were included in the previous year. It instead features a more detailed advertisement for his hymn book collections with a wide variety of options available to the purchaser:

> A Selection of PSALM AND HYMN TUNES from the best Authors, in three or four parts; adapted principally to Dr. Watts' Hymns and Psalms, and to Mr. Rippon's Selection of Hymns. Including (in a greater variety than any other volume extant) the most approved compositions which are used in London and in the different congregations throughout England; also many original tunes never before printed. The whole forming a publication of above two hundred hymn tunes. Price 5s. bound in sheep; paper hot pressed, and bound in calf at 6s. superfine paper 6s. 6d.

[227] Music, 'Baptist Church Music'. [228] Ibid.

> Those who purchase, of Mr. R. six copies of either sort of the Tune books, may have a seventh gratis.[229]

The advert is followed by a two-page alphabetical list of the names of all the tunes contained in the edition. Two and a half pages of the ten-page list are occupied by the advertisement for Rippon's hymnbook, which is the largest space taken up by a single advertisement in the entire *Register*. The hymnbooks were clearly becoming the major part of Rippon's publishing output. In 1790 the works were available in London, Bristol, and Leeds, but by the time of the 1791 list, they were also advertised as available in Sheffield, Edinburgh, Dublin, Boston, Philadelphia, New York, Baltimore, and Charleston.

Another crucial factor in Rippon's increasingly commercial publishing outfit was the multiple options for paper quality and bindings listed in the advert. As David Pearce explains, 'the London bookseller John Brindley, who supplied luxury bindings to numerous wealthy customers during the middle of the eighteenth century, advertised that his shop in New Bond Street always stocked 'sets [of the Classics] kept ready bound in various curious bindings', to make 'very proper presents for young gentlemen pursuing their studies'.[230] Rippon did not offer any of his other publications in this range of bindings, suggesting that the continued commercial viability of his hymnbook editions allowed him to stock them as Brindley did his classics. The range of options available to the customer attests to the demand for the work, but they also show that Rippon either had the capacity to print and bind these works himself or that he maintained consistent professional networks with printers and binders in London. Either way, the practice of offering alternative paper and binding shows the vestry was fulfilling the roles of publisher, bookseller, and binder, activities that Rippon continued to develop as his business grew.

9.2 The Society for Promoting Religious Knowledge

Rippon was a key figure in the Society for Promoting Religious Knowledge (the Book Society), which provided further opportunity to build on his

---

[229] Rippon, *Baptist Annual Register*, p. 326. [230] Pearson, 'Bookbinding', p. 505.

monopoly over hymnbook sales within the Baptist community. Rippon gave sermons for the society and wrote and published a brief history in *A Discourse on the Origin and Progress for the Society for Promoting Religious Knowledge among the Poor* (1803); this contained detailed information on the choice and distribution of books to Baptist ministers, clergy, congregations, and parishioners. The aim of the society was to distribute religious books among the poor, often given freely, but also to lend to readers who could exchange borrowed books for others after having proved they had read and understood the works.[231] These aims dovetailed seamlessly with those of commercial publishers, as maximising the production and distribution of books was as important for the spread of Christianity as it was for publishers' profits.

While promoting Richard Baxter's *Call to the Unconverted* (1658), Rippon celebrates the converting potential of a religious text alongside the quantity of copies published and thus the inevitable commercial concerns that accompanied large scale religious publishing: 'Six brothers in one family were converted by it. Twenty thousand copies of it were printed in about a year by the author's consent, besides many thousands, near the same time, in *pirated* impressions, "which poor men STOLE", Mr Baxter says, "for lucre's sake"'.[232] In the same text Rippon also boasts of the large print runs of Joseph Allein's *Alarm to the Unconverted* (1671), which sold twenty thousand copies under its original title and fifty thousand twenty years later in its second iteration as *The Sure Guide to Heaven* (1691). He then waxed lyrical about the society's own distribution of Isaac Watts' *Psalms and Hymns*, published by Rippon himself:

> If we may appreciate their value, in any measure, by the numbers of them we have distributed, forty thousand hymns, and forty thousand psalms, will give them the rank above any other human compositions in all our catalogue [...] To no denomination of protestants, of any note, among whom the English language is vernacular, have these sacred compositions been confined. Humble cottages, rustic barns,

---

[231] See Rivers, 'Evangelical Tract Society'. [232] Rippon, *Discourse*, p. 19.

> decent meeting houses, and capacious tabernacles, are not
> the only temples which have been made vocal by his lays, or
> whose worshippers soar in his songs.[233]

Most of the works detailed in *A Discourse* were already established bestsellers that were widely available having gone through multiple print runs before their addition to the society's selection. Isaac Watts' *Psalms and Hymns* was no exception and had already been in print in some form since 1707. However, the most up-to-date and readily available versions of Watts' hymns were those arranged and published by Rippon. As with the *Baptist Annual Register*, Rippon positioned his hymnbooks as the only option for Baptist congregations in a key genre for Baptist readers.

The use of periodical publishing to support other publishing efforts was nothing new, of course. Richard Sher's seminal study of Scottish Enlightenment publishing describes the late eighteenth-century book trade as one in which 'the leading British book review journals were closely intertwined with the system of publishing that was dominated by a handful of powerful figures in the book trade'.[234] He details the self-serving journalism of publishers who edited and procured journals to surreptitiously promote their own works, securing what 'was in effect free advertising, at a time when newspaper publishers were feeling increased pressure to use more space for advertisements that generated income'.[235] Rippon's approach differed from Sher's handful of powerful figures in that he did not have to call on favours from associates or disguise his publishing activity in anonymous journals: his clerical authority established him as a tastemaker for both his congregation and his readers.

9.3 Conclusion

In addition to his influential position within the Baptist community, Rippon was also a canny book trade operative. He understood not only publishing and bookselling but also how to deploy the promotional tools at his disposal to sell his books to local and international markets for sacred music and literature. The use of his position as editor and publisher of key Baptist

[233] Ibid., pp. 34–35. [234] Sher, *Enlightenment*, p. 366. [235] Ibid, p. 365.

literature differed again from the exploitation of book review journals as, rather than simply suggesting appropriate up-to-date reading for individuals, it recruited the moral imperatives of the Baptist clergy and early evangelical tract societies to encourage the purchase of large quantities of works to distribute among poorer members of the church and prospective converts.

Rippon's position within the Baptist movement created unique opportunities for the development of a publishing business outside traditional book trade centres. His editorial control of the *Baptist Annual Register* and *A Discourse* provided powerful promotional tools to facilitate the wide commercial distribution of his published works. Rippon's commercial skills went much further than the above examples; he continued to exploit conventional marketing techniques throughout his publishing career, developing personalisation options, money off deals, advertisements, stock lists, and catalogues, all of which are consistent with the innovative marketing strategies of people working in all sorts of different trades.

10 Diversity in the Book Trades: Ann Ireland (1751–1843) of Leicester by John Hinks[236]

10.1 A Bookselling Dynasty

Ann Ireland, part of a prominent printing and bookselling dynasty, ran an outstanding and diverse business in the centre of Leicester. During the mid eighteenth century, Leicester was 'rapidly emerging from the dullness and slowness of the small market town to a state more important'.[237] Like other provincial towns, Leicester experienced economic and cultural 'improvements' at this time, including the arrival in 1740 of the town's first printer, Matthew Unwin.[238] Unwin died in 1749, leaving no printer in Leicester until John Gregory arrived from Derbyshire in 1752, founding the first local newspaper, the *Leicester Journal*, in 1753.[239] The trade grew steadily until 1800, when there were ten printers and ten booksellers.[240]

Two branches of the Ireland family practised in the city.[241] The elder John Ireland was trading as a printer by 1760. He died in 1776, leaving sums of money to both of his nephews, who were also his apprentices: John (1747–1810) and George (1750–1786). Several properties were left in trust to provide an income for his widow, Elizabeth; she also ran her late husband's business for a time with the help of her nephew, John. Both George and John went on to trade separately in Leicester, as booksellers and printers. This chapter focuses on one of these two branches, and particularly on George's widow, Ann Ireland, and her impressive book trade business. Widowed in her mid-thirties, Ann took over her late husband's shop in the Market Place and turned it into one of Leicester's

---

[236] The editors are grateful to the estate of John Hinks for permission to publish this piece and would like to thank Sarah Griffin, Rare Books Librarian at York Minster Library and Archives, for her assistance finalising references.

[237] See Thompson, *History*, p. 82.   [238] See Hinks, *Coming*.

[239] See Hinks, 'John Gregory'.   [240] Hinks and Bell, 'Book Trade'.

[241] I am grateful to the late Norman Harrison for fruitful discussions about the Ireland family.

most important book trade businesses, developing and diversifying with outstanding ability and imagination.

10.2 Generational Shifts

George Ireland had been an important bookseller, printer, and printseller, and established Leicester's first circulating library in 1778.[242] When he died, aged thirty-four, in 1786, the *Leicester Journal* described him as 'a very honest industrious man, [who] left a wife and two children to lament their irreparable loss'.[243] The survival of his business and the security of his wife and children, George (aged thirteen) and Elizabeth, must have been the father's main concerns as he approached the end of his life. His will, made very shortly before his death, sets out detailed provisions to ensure a sound future for both the business and the family:

> And my mind and will is that my said Wife do carry on my several businesses of Bookseller, Bookbinder, and Printer during the minority of my son George Ireland (whom I would have brought up to my said businesses) the better to enable my said Wife in the meantime to maintain and support herself and Family [...].[244]

Ann Ireland, likely an active participant in the business, was clearly regarded by her husband as far more than a mere 'caretaker' during the minority of their son. The will further specifies that, when their son comes of age (at twenty-one), he and his mother are to enter into partnership 'and jointly carry on for their material benefit [...] my said several businesses during their joint lives if my said Wife shall so long continue my Widow'.[245] Further detailed provisions cover the possibility of Ann's remarriage before her son reached twenty-one. George also left some money to his mother and to his daughter, both named Elizabeth.

---

[242] *Leicester Journal*, 17 October 1778. [243] *Leicester Journal*, 13 May 1786.
[244] Record Office for Leicestershire, Leicester and Rutland, PR/T/1786/94.
[245] Ibid.

Ann left no trace of her trading activities until her husband died and she took over the business as well as George's only known apprentice, Samuel Adams. The son of the Loughborough bookseller William Adams, Samuel had been bound to George on 3 May 1782 and was one of the witnesses to his master's will. The record of his freedom, on 12 June 1790, describes him as the apprentice of 'George Ireland, late of Leicester, bookseller, and afterwards with his widow'; in 1792 Ann herself directly became 'master' to a second apprentice printer, Richard Slatter.[246]

When she took over the business, Ann placed the following announcement in the *Leicester Journal* on 20 May 1786:

> Ann Ireland widow of George Ireland, bookseller, printer, bookbinder and printseller, takes the Liberty of informing the friends of her late Husband and the public in general, that the Business in its several branches, will be carried on by her as usual – a continuance of their favours will be thankfully acknowledged.[247]

However, within six months she was forced to move to another shop:

> Ann Ireland (widow of the late Geo. Ireland) Printer, Bookseller, Binder and Printseller, Begs leave to inform her Friends and the Public, that being under the necessity of leaving her former situation, has now removed to the house, late Mr. Cooper's, Apothecary, opposite the Assembly-Room [...] where the several Businesses above-mentioned will be carried on, and all favours thankfully acknowledged [...].[248]

The advertisement also mentions that the circulating library now contains two thousand volumes and that catalogues are available. The reason for

---

[246] Hartopp, *Register*, pp. 59, 461. [247] *Leicester Journal*, 20 May 1786.
[248] *Leicester Journal*, 14 October 1786.

The People of Print 77

Ann's move had been indicated in an announcement by her nephew, John Ireland, a week earlier:

> John Ireland, Printer, bookseller and binder Wishes to inform his friends and the public in general that (according to the will of his uncle, Mr. John Ireland) he has entered upon the well accustomed shop opposite the Conduit in the Market Place; where he intends carrying on the printing, Bookselling and stationary business in all their various branches [...] He returns his sincere thanks to his numerous friends for their favours at his late shop in Gallowtree-gate, and humbly hopes he shall experience a continuance of them in his new situation [...][249]

John Ireland, presumably following the recent death of his aunt, Elizabeth Ireland (widow of the elder John Ireland), now had a claim on the premises in the Market Place in which Ann was trading (and probably also living), forcing her to move elsewhere. She made a sound decision in moving to premises across from the Assembly Rooms, which attracted county gentry, professional people, and wealthier townsfolk. This was a fashionable and potentially lucrative location for her bookshop, printing office, and circulating library and all three businesses thrived.

10.3 Development and Diversification

Ann had almost certainly been an active part of her husband's successful business. After George's death, Ann developed it further, diversifying to an impressive extent. This pattern continued when she operated in partnership with her son, creating a thriving and wide-ranging concern. Ann traded successfully as a bookseller and circulating librarian, and also as a very competent printer. During the next few years, her advertisements indicate a fashionable range of goods for sale, including music, musical instruments, fine art prints, theatre tickets, new periodicals 'direct from London', in addition to the standard fare of new and second-hand books, school-books,

---

[249] *Leicester Journal*, 7 October 1786.

stationery, and patent medicines. From time to time she also advertised for journeymen printers and book-binders; this indicates that there was enough work to recruit outside help.[250]

An important piece of evidence for the diversity of Ann's business is a single surviving book-sale catalogue, dating from 1789:

> A catalogue of Books, containing a great variety in most languages, arts and sciences; which will begin to be sold (for ready money) at the prices printed in the Catalogue; on Friday, July 17th, 1789, at the shop of Ann Ireland, Bookseller and Printer, opposite the Assembly Room, Leicester (who gives full value for any library or parcel of books). Catalogues may be had of the Neighbouring Booksellers, and of Mr. Crowder, Pater-Noster-Row, London.[251]

The catalogue provides detailed evidence of Ann's stock and services:

> At the Place of Sale may be had, Bibles and Common Prayer Books, in Morocco or other Bindings. Account Books and Ledgers of all Sorts, Rul'd or Plain, and Bound to any Pattern or Order. Stationary ware of all kinds. A Capital Collection of Maps and Prints. Magazines, Reviews, and all other periodical publications. Blank Warrants and Precedents for Coroners, High-Constables, Justices Clerks etc. etc. Music, Rul'd Music Paper, Harpsichord lessons, new songs, with every Article in the Musical Line. Letter Cases, Morocco, Spanish and Common Leather, with Straps or Clasps. Schoolmasters, and Country Shopkeepers, may be supplied with School books of all sorts – as also with Copy and Account Books, Quills, Pens, Black and Red Ink,

---

[250] Examples: *Leicester Journal*, 25 October 1788; 24 September 1790; 4 October 1793; 30 December 1796; 27 October 1797.

[251] Ireland, *Catalogue*, title page.

> Writing Paper of the best Quality etc. etc. On the Lowest
> Terms. Printing in General, executed with Neatness and
> Dispatch – And Books bound in a Neat and Firm Manner, or
> in Elegant Bindings, on Reasonable Terms.[252]

The mention of a range of musical items indicates Ann's willingness to diversify the business and her engagement with the interests of the local community. Leicester at this time had a fine reputation for musical performance and innovation.[253] Moreover, the detail in the list above indicates the care and comprehensiveness with which she advertised her stock: she promotes not just letter cases but those in 'Morocco, Spanish and Common Leather, with Straps or Clasps'. The 1789 catalogue consists of 102 octavo pages, listing 2,402 books, arranged by size and then by language or subject. A number of works in Latin, Greek, and French are included. Dr Johnson's edition of certain poets is listed, 'new and sewed in marble paper' at 2s. 6d. each. The most expensive book (one of only a few new books listed) is priced at eighteen shillings, while at the other end of the range, there is a selection of odd volumes and miscellaneous titles at sixpence each; most books are priced between ninepence and five shillings. The condition of many volumes is noted in terms such as 'very neat', 'fair', and similar, while a few are described with commendable honesty as 'not quite perfect', 'wants a cover', 'bad condition', and suchlike. Ann clearly registered the importance to customers, and to the reputation of her growing business, not just of providing an alluring array of products but of a frank assessment of them. By 1800, the circulating library had grown to some three thousand volumes, another of Ann's successful business developments.

Ann was also the printer of a number of books, including an important text written by the celebrated local Baptist minister, missionary, and leading oriental scholar, William Carey (1761–1834). *An Enquiry into the Obligations of Christians to Use Means for the Conversion of the Heathens* (1792) comprises eighty-seven octavo pages, neatly printed with tasteful decoration and several tables. The high status of this work in Baptist circles is indicated by the fact that

---

[252] Ibid., p. 1.   [253] See Gardiner, *Music*.

it is still in print. The Baptist Missionary Society, founded by Carey, has published several facsimile editions of Ann's original printing, including one issued in 1934 to mark the centenary of Carey's death. The imprint indicates that Ann's trade network clearly included not only local booksellers and printers but also leading publisher-booksellers in London, a connection of vital importance to the success of an ambitious provincial book-trade business.[254]

Radicalism and dissenting religion often went hand in hand; Leicester had strong communities of Baptists and Unitarians, some of whom held radical political views. Many local book-trade people tended towards radical opinions but, although Ann published an important Baptist text, she was a member of the Church of England and her son's political activities for the Corporation clearly identify him as a Tory.[255] Leicester was a politically divided borough. The Corporation was staunchly Tory and was becoming a notorious example of municipal corruption. On the other hand, the town was also known as 'Radical Leicester', a reputation which endured into the mid-nineteenth century and beyond.[256]

10.4 Conclusion: Later Years

Ann Ireland's final extant printed work is Edward Pyke's *Hymn and Songs in Praise of Jesus Christ*, an octavo volume of 136 pages, probably printed in the first five years of the nineteenth century. When Ann ceased trading is not known, though it seems likely that she ran the business herself until she retired. It was usually known as 'Ireland and Son' between 1791 and 1811, though references to 'Ann(e) Ireland' and 'Mrs Ireland' are also found during the same period.[257] The latest extant book carrying the 'Ireland and Son' imprint is dated 1800.[258] Ann's son, George, was kept busy with his civic duties and his own businesses. He was a prominent citizen of Leicester, being made a councilman in 1802, chamberlain in 1805, and mayor in

---

[254] Feather, *Provincial*, pp. 1–11. [255] See Hinks, 'Some Radical'.
[256] See Patterson, *Radical Leicester*.
[257] See *Leicester Journal*, 2 September 1796; *Universal Directories*, 1791 to 1794; *Weston's Directory*, 1794; *Holden's Directories* 1805 to 1811.
[258] Anon., *Concise Thoughts*.

1821.[259] Despite being a partner in the business with his mother, George seems to have been only peripherally involved in its day-to-day running. However, several books that he printed are listed in the ESTC, and two apprentices were bound to him, perhaps nominally as he was the male partner.[260] George died, aged fifty-three, on 23 December 1826, predeceasing Ann by seventeen years. Although no evidence has been found for the final years of the business, it certainly survived until at least 1811, after which it ceases to be listed in local directories or other sources. Ann died on 13 January 1843, at the age of ninety-three, having spent her later years living, very near where her business had been located, with several of her grandchildren. She is buried with her husband in the churchyard of her parish church, St Martin's, which later became Leicester Cathedral.[261]

---

[259] Hartopp, *Roll*, p. 188.
[260] For example, *Traits on Human Woe* (1780) by 'a Spectator'; Thomas, *Observations*; Deacon, *New Composition*. Several of the imprints indicate continuing connections with London printers and booksellers, and some in Oxford and Cambridge, for example, (Anon.) *Ecclesiastes, in Three Parts*. For George Ireland's apprentices, see Hartopp, *Register*, vol. 2, pp. 512, 132.
[261] Hartopp, *Roll*, p. 188.

11 'Laugh when you must, be candid when you can': The Concealed Resistance of the Radical Printer Winifred Gales (1761–1839)
by Adam James Smith

11.1 Introduction

In Sheffield, during the summer of 1794, a heavily pregnant Winifred Gales (1761–1839) was interrogated for hours by a panel of magistrates investigating the alleged relationship between her husband – printer and newspaper editor Joseph Gales – and Henry Yorke. The magistrates were in pursuit of Yorke following the publication of a pamphlet which included the transcript of a speech he had given which they considered to be seditious. Yorke was the son of a sugar plantation owner and an enslaved woman of colour and, as Steven and Neil Kay put it, 'a crowd puller'.[262] The authorities believed the pamphlet had been printed by the press operating out of Hartshead Square, Sheffield: a press run by Joseph Gales and his wife, Winifred. They had received reports that Yorke had been lodging with the Gales in their home – reports which, in fact, are now documented as accurate.

Recounting the episode over a decade later in her handwritten *Recollections* – which she wrote at some point between 1815 and 1839 – Winifred described how, though physically exhausted from the pregnancy and the stress caused by the looming threat of arrest, she was determined to prevent her testimony being used to convict her husband or their friend Yorke. In her account of the interrogation, Winifred imagines a dialogue playing out in her mind's eye, between the apostrophised speakers, 'Fear' and 'Resolution':

> Besides, said Fear, if you cross them they will send you to London to be examined by the Privy Council. Let them do their worst said Resolution, I will not burthen my

[262] Kay and Kay, *How Great a Crime*, p. 124.

conscience by incriminating this young Man [Yorke], which
I may, unknowingly do. I determined to be silent.[263]

Winifred's account aligns closely with a literary tradition of female life-writing, in which captives maintain silence under interrogation by male captors. A well-known instance of such writing is the testimony of Anne Askew, who 'became one of the more famous of the Tudor Protestant martyrs, immortalised through the publication of what are purported to be autobiographical descriptions of her imprisonment, trials and condemnation, as well as various parts of her correspondence'.[264] According to Winifred, when asked about the pamphlet, she responded,

> 'I have read it'.
> 'You perhaps saw it in Manuscript'.
> 'No'.
> 'It is said to have been printed in Mr Gales's Office. You may have seen it there perhaps?'
> 'No, my business does not lie in the office. I have a large family'.[265]

Winifred's interrogators did not press the point, accepting her word that, as a mother of four, her sphere of activity was wholly domestic.[266] Upon concluding her interrogation, the magistrates moved on to interviewing the workers from the Hartshead Press print rooms:

> 'You', said they to a sturdy illiterate Press Man, 'you must recollect printing this Pamphlet'. 'Very loike, Sir, but as I have no larning and cannot read, I doesn't know'. They

---

[263] Gales, *Recollections*, p. 71. [264] Hickerson, 'Ways of Lying', p. 50.
[265] Gales, *Recollections*, p. 72.
[266] Winifred Gales was not the first female person of print to avoid prosecution because of the assumption that it was unlikely that a woman would be motivated by political commitments. For instance, see Farmer, 'Ann Griffin', pp. 38–52.

> laughed very heartily at the idea of a Printer, not being able to read.[267]

It was not true, however, that the management of the Hartshead Press was entirely Winifred's husband's domain, just as the complete ignorance of her Press Man was likely also feigned. Indeed, shortly after this interrogation, Joseph would flee to America as a fugitive of the law, and Winifred would take charge of the business entirely. She later wrote:

> Contemplate my dear children, the trying situation of your Mother. My husband gone! A printing office with 16 hands in it – a newspaper to edit – a store in full business – four infants, i.e. very young children, and myself within a few months of adding another to the number![268]

Even prior to this, Winifred's business had very much been in the offices of the Hartshead Press. With their repeated assertions of her agency, and detail about her varied activities, Winifred's hand-written *Recollections* have helped scholars reconstruct her role at the Hartshead Press. The *Recollections* take the form of a handwritten diary with some annotations from Joseph. They do not make any claim to being written for publication. Indeed, the intended audience is for the most part unclear, although Winifred does occasionally address her children directly.

Winifred was also a novelist, took an active role in managing the Hartshead Press, and supported Joseph's unmarried sisters in managing their own bookselling and stationery business. Winifred does seem, however, to have been shrewdly practised in taking advantage of gendered assumptions to obfuscate her agency, particularly when that agency was connected to activities that might be prosecutable by law.[269] As Michael Daly has observed, 'it seems, ironically, to have been the contemporary male perception that middling-sort women should devote themselves to the plain and unproductive labour of the "separate sphere" of housework that

---

[267] Gales, *Recollections*, p. 72.
[268] Qtd in Kay and Kay, *How Great a Crime*, p. 139. [269] See Barker, *Business*.

actually saved her from prosecution'.[270] This essay foregrounds the key strategy by which Winifred concealed her agency. It also highlights how this strategy, combined with the fact that she was both a woman and a person of print operating in a regional context, has meant that little attention has been paid to Winifred's active role in managing and ultimately sustaining the press.[271] By delineating Winifred's considerable contributions to the Hartshead Press, and examining the ways in which these contributions were hidden, this essay also models ways we might read against autobiographical claims made by female people of print and recover the labour they themselves may have sought to conceal. It also exemplifies some of the ways that the obfuscatory tactics deployed by female people of print have inadvertently hidden their agency from scholars of print and book history.

11.2 Winifred and the Press

Winifred Marshall met Joseph Gales when he was apprenticed to a printer and bookseller, Mr Tomlinson, who operated in the Nottinghamshire town of Newark. Tomlinson was also a dealer of carpets and wallpaper, an auctioneer and appraiser, and the custodian of a circulating library. Winifred regularly used the library, and it was here that she met Tomlinson's apprentice, Joseph.[272] She was the daughter of John and Elizabeth Marshall, who owned a considerable estate (Winifred's grandmother's cousin was Lord Melbourne). The two decided to establish a printing business in Sheffield, using Winifred's inheritance, Joseph's savings, and a set of loans from Joseph's London contacts (loans which, some years later, Winifred would be independently responsible for settling).

Joseph quickly got to work, forging connections with the freemen cutlers of Sheffield and laying the groundwork for what would ultimately become the Sheffield Society for Constitutional Information and the Friends of Peace and Reform: radical groups agitating for parliamentary reform and better representation in government for the labouring classes.[273] Winifred,

---

[270] Daly, 'From Sheffield', p. 90. [271] Smith, 'The Newspaper', pp. 71–89.
[272] Ibid., p. 73. [273] Ibid., p. 75.

meanwhile, soon became pregnant. Their first child, born in March 1785, died after only a few hours and the birth itself almost killed Winifred. A second child, Joseph, was born in April 1786. During this period, Winifred also wrote her first novel, *The History of Lady Emma Melcombe and Her Family*, which was published by the Hartshead press the following year. Proudly stating on its frontispiece that it has been written 'By a female', the novel seeks to make an intervention that readers might now justifiably recognise as feminist:

> Man have ever been held infinitely superior to Women, in respect to literary abilities ... Yet we are indebted, within these few years, to the exertions of a GRAHAM, a BARBAULD, a MOORE, a SEWARD, a COWLEY, and a BURNET, to lessen, in some degree, the distinction between the sexes, as writers.[274]

Winifred's novel tells the story of a widow and her two children who are befriended by the benevolent, eccentric aristocrat Lady Montgomery. It is a tale of female solidarity, taking place almost exclusively outside of the male social sphere. By naming celebrated women writers such as Anna Laetitia Barbauld and Hannah More at the outset, Winifred positions her novel within a tradition of women's writing seeking to demonstrate that literary ability is not contingent on sex. Winifred insinuates instead that such assumptions are born of what Mary Wollstonecraft would soon identify as 'false education' to which women are subjected under patriarchy.[275] The novel also bears on its frontispiece the motto, 'Laugh when you must, be candid when you can', a philosophy which

---

[274] Gales, *Lady Emma Melcombe*, p. xii. The women listed here are all poets, some of whom were also playwrights and literary critics: Janet Graham (1723–1805), Anna Laetitia Barbauld (1742–1825), Hannah Moore (1745–1833), Anna Seward (1742–1809), and Hannah Cowley (1742–1809). Burnet may refer to prayer-book owner Elizabeth Burnet (1661–1709), or be a variant spelling of Burney, and refer to the novelist, diarist, and playwright Frances Burney (1752–1840).

[275] Wollstonecraft, *Rights*, p. 132.

would also come to underpin Winifred's self-concealing strategies as a radical printer and bookseller.

11.3 Winifred Gales and Revolutionary Sheffield

On June 9 1787, the Hartshead Press published the first issue of *The Sheffield Register*. The paper, which quickly became a platform for radicalism, reform, and abolitionist activism, also regularly published letters and poems attributed to local literary women. According to Hannah Barker, the *Register* is remembered for its flagrant commitment to radical change on behalf of a readership it considered to be downtrodden and disenfranchised. The recollections of Jewitt, a contemporary operating in Sheffield at the time, recognises Winfred's contribution to the *Register*: 'Mrs Gales was a very clever woman being greatly considered as the editor on Gales leaving Sheffield'.[276] As Kay and Kay note, 'we can only speculate on just how involved [Winifred] was in the editorial work of the newspaper, but it is reasonable to assume she was very hands-on, even if she could not be seen to be so'.[277] Indeed, Winifred took great care to maintain plausible deniability at the expense of gaining recognition for her own varied and extensive labour.

Even when describing the *Register* in her *Recollections*, Winifred centres the role of her husband, Joseph. She characterises Joseph not as a willing agitator but as a reluctant and moderate man of the people compelled to make a stand. According to Winifred, Joseph's ambition had been to provide a voice for workers and artisans in Sheffield. She claimed that his readers were 'glad to find their grievances so moderately stated, and so respectfully submitted, and the printer was credited [first] for putting their demands into good language, and later for the propriety with which they were addressed'.[278] In Winifred's telling, Joseph was simply a 'good man' inspired to action through sympathy, empathy, and a strong sense of social justice.[279] Of course, this representation simultaneously conceals any partisan or entrepreneurial imperative on behalf of Winifred and Joseph. As I have argued elsewhere though, 'the impossibility of anonymity in regional

---

[276] Jewitt cited in Kay and Kay, *How Great a Crime*, p. 9.   [277] Ibid., p. 9.
[278] Gales cited in Ashton, *Iron and Steel*, p. 205.   [279] Gales, *Recollections*, p. 45.

printing made it genuinely dangerous for Gales or [James] Montgomery to be overly explicit about their intentions as printers, as both learnt to their cost'.[280]

Michael Daly characterises Winifred's *Recollections* as being largely written to justify the Gales' 'involvement in reform politics as moderates', noting that Joseph is portrayed as a 'cultured moderate whose concern was to quietly promote parliamentary reform and the rights of the working man', whilst Winifred describes the *Sheffield Register* 'as a mild and reasonable voice for the grievances of the Sheffield artisans'.[281] Even so, there are clear parallels between the moderate strategies Winifred attributes to her husband and the strategies she describes herself adopting in moments of extremis.

11.3 The Resistance of Winifred Gales

One extraordinary episode of Winifred's *Recollections* relates a dramatic event at sea. While escaping Britain on the 'William and Henry', a ship full of fellow emigrants, the vessel was captured by a privateer who styled himself Captain Hutchins. With Joseph incapacitated below deck, suffering severe seasickness, it was Winifred who engaged the captain and proved successful not only in persuading him to let their ship go but also in getting him to give them extra provisions as compensation for the inconvenience he had caused:

> Captain Hutchins requested the Lieutenant to reach the Letter Bags, which he did and deliberately began to open the letters. I smiled, perhaps shrewdly, for Hutchins caught the involuntary expression, and asked what amused me. 'Your honourable profession, which rises every moment in my estimation – what! Open private letters, – explore family secrets – interfere with confidential communications – I am sorry to have witnessed it'. With a raised voice and heightened colour, he drew his chair near me, and said, we must converse together. 'Do you recollect you are a Captive'

[280] Smith, 'The Newspaper', p. 87. [281] Daly, 'From Sheffield', pp. 46, 58, 47.

> 'Yes' I replied cheerfully 'but if we had but one stern chaser, you could not have called me so'. A little more passed in good humour, and the right they had to capture the William and Henry was seriously discussed – Finally, he waived his privilege, convinced that we had no munitions of War on Board, the plea which was urged as a pretence. 'And now, Madam, what can I do for you and your children, as compensation for detaining you?' With courteous thanks, for his conduct demanded it, I replied, 'We have no Loaf Sugar – no Molases – no Flour'.[282]

In this tale, Winifred triumphs over the dangerous privateer captain by first embarrassing him, drawing attention to his less-than-chivalrous behaviour (his colour becomes 'heightened'), then by winning him over with polite 'good humour', and then ultimately by subjecting his actions to 'serious' discussion, all while her husband is out of action below deck. Whether or not these events happened as Winifred describes, the narrative account confirms an awareness of the ways gendered assumptions could be mobilised – she was able to exploit the captain's aversion to being understood as having acted in an ungentlemanly manner – and a faith in the power of reason to resolve conflict. Her male partner, Joseph, is incapacitated with sea-sickness, rendered passive, and, according to the logics Winifred is resisting, feminised. It is therefore down to her, a woman, to take on the active, typically masculine role, and confront the privateer captain. She does so through the commanding application of reason, which, Winifred shows here, is no more purely the domain of men than writing. At the same time, she is cheerfully prepared to play the role of a charming, amiable companion, defusing the situation by exchanging the pleasure of her feminine company. This ability to harness gendered assumptions while asserting her agency is a manoeuvre she deploys time and again throughout her career.

Winifred's *Recollections* also reveal, however, that when there was no alternative, and no hope of hiding her involvement in revolutionary machinations, she was not afraid to stand her ground. For instance, when the

---

[282] Gales, *Recollections*, p. 137.

authorities came for her, pursuing her husband with an arrest warrant, she refused to comply easily, instead calmly informing them that she would come when she had finished her tea:

> Mr Wilkinson the Rector of Trinity Church, Col. Athorpe, and Dr Zouch wish to see you at the Tontine Inn! 'Well!' I answered somewhat impatiently, I confess, 'they must know where I live'. 'Yes, Madam' he replied 'but they sit as Magistrates and had me say they invite, rather than command your attendance'. I told him when I had taken my Tea, then ready, I would go, for it was early in July, and the day long.[283]

Winifred was far from a peripheral figure in the story of the Hartshead press. Throughout her varied work at the press, as a printer, editor, entrepreneur, and most explicitly as an author, she championed the cause of women, insisting that they are reasoning and capable creatures who should be understood as such. At the same time, she knew how to take advantage of patriarchal assumptions about the interests and abilities of women, repeatedly alluding censure and conviction, and ensuring the persistence of both the Hartshead press and its radical message by welcoming the obfuscation of her agency.

---

[283] Ibid., p. 69.

Abbreviations

BBTI British Book Trades Index
ESTC English Short Title Catalogue
ODNB *Oxford Dictionary of National Biography Online*
PROB Records of the Prerogative Court of Canterbury
SP State Papers Office

Bibliography

Addison, J., and R. Steele. (1711). *The Spectator*. 1 March.

Alderson, B. (1999). New Playthings and Gigantick Histories: The Nonage of English Children's Books. *The Princeton University Library Chronicle*, 60(2), 178–95.

Alexiou, A., Roberto, R. eds. (2022). *Women in Print*. Oxford: Peter Lang.

Anon. (1768). *An Accurate Depiction and History of the Cathedral and Metropolitical Church of St. Peter, York*. York: Printed by A. Ward, for T. Wilson, C. Etherington, W. Tesseyman, J. Todd, and H. Sotheran, and D. Peek.

(1712/13). Advertisements and Notices. *Evening Post*, 23 March. Seventeenth and Eighteenth Century Burney Newspapers Collection, Gale Z2000181694.

(1712/13). Advertisements and Notices. *Evening Post*, 24–27 March. Seventeenth and Eighteenth Century Burney Newspapers Collection, Gale Z2001368640.

(1714). Advertisements and Notices. *Post Boy*, 24–27 July. Seventeenth and Eighteenth Century Burney Newspapers Collection, Gale Z2001405014.

(1718). *At the Queen's Head Tavern in Pater-Noster Row, on Thursday the Third Day of April, 1718 Exactly at Four a-clock in the Afternoon; the Following Lists of Copies Belonging to the Late Mr. John Nicholson, Bookseller, Will Be Disposed of by Auction to the Highest Bider*. London.

(1719). *At the Queen's Head Tavern in Pater-Noster-Row, on Thursday the Nineteenth Day of March, 1718, Exactly at Three a Clock in the Afternoon; the Following Copies, and Parts of Copies, of the Late Mr. John Nicholson, Bookseller, deceas'd, Will Be dispos'd of by Auction to the Highest Bidder*. London. ESTC 006397639.

(1720). *At the Queen's Head Tavern in Pater-Noster-Row, on Tuesday, 26th July, ... the Following Copies and Parts of Copies of Mr. A. Churchill, will be Disposed of by Auction*. London. ESTC 006397639.

(1767). *A Catalogue of the Copies and Shares of Copies of Jacob and Richard Tonson, Esqrs*. London. ESTC 006397783.

(1743). *The Child's New Play-Thing*, 2nd ed. London: Printed for M. Cooper at the Globe in Pater-Noster Row.

(1800). *Concise Thoughts on the Game Laws*, by a Leicestershire Free-Holder. Leicester: Printed by Ireland and Son, and sold by C. Chapple, London.

(1712/13). *Daily Courant*, 23 March. *Burney Newspapers Collection*, Gale Z2000181694.

(1715). *The Devout Christian's Companion*. London: Printed for E. Curll at the Dial and Bible against St. Dunstan's Church in Fleetstreet; K. Sanger in Bartholomew-Close; and B. Barker and C. King in Westminster-Hall.

(1791). *Ecclesiastes, in Three Parts: A New Translation, with a Paraphrase*. Leicester: Printed by George Ireland, and sold by J. Fletcher, in Oxford; J. Nicholson, in Cambridge, and W. Lowndes, Fleet Street, London.

(1716). *Exercitia Latina*. London: A Bettesworth, R. Smith, T. Ward, and T. Bickerton. ESTC 006012079.

(1720). *Exercitia Latina*. London: J. Nicholson, R. Parker, and A Bettesworth. ESTC 006318706.

(1728). From Hampton Court to Lord Chancellor: Enclosing a copy of *Mist's Journal* of Saturday Last Desiring His Lordship to Read the Libels. 26 August. MS Records Assembled by the State Paper Office SP 36/8/1/ f. 61.

(1759). *The Genuine Account of the Trial of Eugene Aram, for the Murder of Daniel Clark*. York: Printed by A. Ward, for C. Etherington, bookseller in Coney-Street.

(1721). H.M. to Townshend. 30 May. MS Records Assembled by the State Paper Office SP 35/26 f. 186.

(1710). *The History of the Two Children in the Wood*. Newcastle: John White.

(1728). A Libel Offered for Publication in *Mist's Journal*, Being a Letter from Amos Duge to Mr. Mist Containing an Account of Persia. 24 August. MS Records Assembled by the State Paper Office SP 36/81/1 f.50.

(1698). *A New Adventure, for Law-Books to be Disposed of by Lot, Wherein all are Gainers [. . .] Thursday, July 21.1698*. London: Dan. Brown and John Nicholson. ESTC 006163550.

(1768). *Nomina Villarum Eboracensium: Or, An Index of all the Towns and Villages in the County of York, and County of the City of York*. York: Printed by A. Ward, in Coney-Street.

(1780). *Traits on Human Woe: By a Spectator*. Leicester: Printed by George Ireland.

(1729). Two documents relating to persons taken into custody on account of the libel published in *Mist's Journal*: (1) a list of prisoners. 20 September. MS Records Assembled by the State Paper Office SP 36/8/2 f. 25.

(1731). *The Use of Human Reason in Religion*. Newcastle upon Tyne: Printed by John White, and sold by Mr Button, Mr Bryson, and Mr Akenhead, Booksellers: Mr Waghorn, and Mr Aisley in Durham; Mr Clarke in Sunderland; Mr Hildyard, Mr Manklin and Mr Hammond in York; Mr Swale in Leeds; Mr Ryles and Mr Ferraby in Hull; Mr Hall and Mr Cook in Carlisle; Mr Mackreith in Lancashire; Mr Ashburn in Kendal; and Mr Midwinter in London.

(1711). *Wit Newly Revived, Being a Book of Riddles*. Newcastle: John White.

Ashton, T. S. (1951). *Iron and Steel in the Industrial Revolution*. Manchester: Manchester University Press.

Axford, J. ([1708]). *Hidden Things Brought to Light, for the Increase in Knowledge, in Reading the Holy Bible*. Newcastle: Printed and sold by John White.

Backus, I. (1777). *A History of New England, with Particular Reference to the Denomination of Christians Called Baptists [. . .] Collected from Most Authentic Records and Writings, Etc*. Boston: Phillip Freeman.

Baker, S. (1959). Henry Fielding's *The Female Husband*: Fact and Fiction. *PMLA*, 74(3), 213–24.

Barker, H. (2006). *The Business of Women: Female Enterprise and Urban Development in Northern England, 1760–1830*. Oxford: Oxford University Press.

  (1998). *Newspapers, Politics, and Public Opinion in Late Eighteenth-Century England*. Oxford: Oxford University Press.

Belanger, T. (1975). Booksellers' Trade Sales, 1718–1768. *The Library*, 5 (30), 281–302.

  (1982). Publishers and Writers in Eighteenth-Century England. In I. Rivers, ed., *Books and Their Readers in Eighteenth-Century England*. Leicester: Leicester University Press, pp. 5–25.

Betterton, T. (1714). *The Amorous Widow; or, Wanton Wife: A Comedy*, 3rd ed. London: Printed by S. Keimer for E. Curll, R. Gosling, K. Sanger, and A. Bettesworth.

Billings, W. M. (1997). A Neglected Treatise: Lewis Kerr's Exposition and the Making of Criminal Law in Louisiana. *Louisiana History: The Journal of the Louisiana Historical Association*, 38(3), 261–86.

Black, J. (1987). An Underrated Journalist: Nathaniel Mist and the Opposition Press during the Whig Ascendency. *British Journal for Eighteenth-Century Studies*, 10(1), 27–41.

Blagden, C. (1951). Booksellers' Trade Sales, 1718–1768. *The Library*, 5(4), 243–57.

Box, M. A., Harvey, D., and Silverthorne, M. (2003). A Diplomatic Transcription of Hume's 'Volunteer Pamphlet' for Archibald Stewart: Political Whigs, Religious Whigs, and Jacobites. *Hume Studies*, 29(2), 223–31.

Brant, C., and Rousseau, G. (2018). Introduction. In C. Brant and G. Rousseau, eds., *Fame and Fortune: Sir John Hill and London Life in the 1750s*. London: Palgrave Macmillan, pp. 1–29.

Bricker, A. (2022). *Libel and Lampoon: Satire in the Courts, 1670–1792*. Oxford: Oxford University Press.

Cannan, P. D. (2004). Early Shakespeare Criticism, Charles Gildon, and the Making of Shakespeare the Playwright-Poet. *Modern Philology*, 102(1), 35–55.

Carey, W. (1792). *An Enquiry into the Obligations of Christians to Use Means for the Conversion of the Heathens*. Leicester, London, and Sheffield: Ann Ireland, and the other Booksellers in Leicester; J. Johnson, St. Paul's Church yard; T. Knott, Lombard Street; R. Dilly, in the Poultry, London; Smith at Sheffield. ESTC T122376.

Carnell, R. (1999). 'It's Not Easy Being Green': Gender and Friendship in Eliza Haywood's Political Periodical. *Eighteenth-Century Studies*, 32(2), 199–215.

　(2018). Protesting the Exclusivity of the Public Sphere: Delarivier Manley's *Examiner*. In J. Batchelor and M. Powell, eds., *Women's Periodicals and Print Culture in Britain, 1690–1820*. Edinburgh: Edinburgh University Press, pp. 153–64.

Christie, I. R. (1962). *Wilkes, Wyvill, and Reform: The Parliamentary Reform Movement in British Politics, 1760–1785*. London: St Martin's Press.

Coker, C. (2018). Gendered Spheres: Theorizing Place in the English Printing House. *The Seventeenth Century*, 33(3), 323–36.

Cowan, B. (2004). Mr. Spectator and the Coffeehouse Public Sphere. *Eighteenth-Century Studies*, 37(3), 345–66.

Cranfield, G. A. (1962). *The Development of the Provincial Newspaper, 1700–1760*. Oxford: Clarendon Press.

Crew, S., Hutchins, J., and Bincham [Bineham]. (1728). Applying for Payment of Expenses Incurred in Arresting and Securing the Printers and Publishers of *Mist's Journal*. MS Records Assembled by the State Paper Office SP 36/9/2/ f. 99.

Crosbie, B. (2020). *Age Relations and Cultural Change in Eighteenth-Century England*. Woodbridge: Boydell and Brewer.

  (2023). Anne Fisher and the Union Street Press: Gender and Print in Eighteenth-Century Newcastle-upon-Tyne. *Archaeologia Aeliana*, 6 (2), 307–19.

  (2018). Provincial Purveyors of Culture: The Print Trade in Eighteenth-Century Newcastle-upon-Tyne. In A. Green and B. Crosbie, eds., *Economy and Culture in North-East England, 1500–1800*. Woodbridge: Boydell and Brewer, pp. 205–29.

Crouzet, F. (1980). Toward an Export Economy: British Exports during the Industrial Revolution. *Explorations in Economic History*, 17, 48–93.

Curtis, L. P. (1932). The First Printer of *Tristram Shandy*. *PMLA*, 47(3), 777–89.

Dally, M. J. (2011). From Sheffield to Raleigh: A Radical Publishing Network in the Age of Revolution. *Sheffield Hallam University Research Archive*, http://shura.shu.ac.uk/4075.

d'Artanville, M. (1716). *Memoirs of Prince Eugene of Savoy*. London: Printed by J. Darby for K. Sanger, and sold by T. Varnam and J. Osborn in Lombard-Street, W. Taylor and A. Bettesworth in Pater-Noster-Row, J. Brown without Temple-Bar, and C. King in Westminster-Hall.

Davies, R. (1868). *A Memoir of the York Press*. London: Nichols and Sons.

Deacon, S. (1784). *A New Composition of Hymns and Poems*. Leicester: Printed for the author, by George Ireland.

Defoe. D. (1989). *A Tour of the Whole Island of Great Britain* (1724–27). P. Rogers, ed. Exeter: Webb and Bower.

Delafaye, C. (1729). Examination of Catherine Nutt. In Examinations of persons upon criminal matters. 19 July. MS Records Assembled by the State Paper Office SP 36/13/115.

Downie, J. A., and T. Cornes, eds. (1992). *Telling People What to Think: Early Eighteenth-Century Periodicals from* The Review *to* The Rambler. London: Routledge.

Eisenstein, E. (1979). *The Printing Press as an Agent of Change*. Cambridge: Cambridge University Press.

Ellis. M. (2009). Coffee-House Libraries in Mid-Eighteenth-Century London. *The Library*, 7th series, 10(1), 3–40.

  (2021). Sociability and Polite Improvement in Addison's Periodicals. In P. Davis, ed., *Joseph Addison: Tercentenary Essays*. Oxford: Oxford University Press, pp. 142–63.

Evelyn, J. (1776). *Silva: Or a Discourse of Forest-Trees, and the propagation of Timber in His Majesty's Dominions*. York: Printed by A. Ward for J. Dodsley, Pall-Mall; T. Cadell, in the Strand; J. Robson, New Bond-Street; and T. Durham, Charing-Cross, London. W. Creech and J. Balfour, Edinburgh.

  (1778). *Terra: A Philosophical Discourse of Earth, Relating to the Culture and Improvement of It for Vegetation, and the Propagation of Plants*. York: Printed by A. Ward, for J. Dodsley, Pall-Mall; T. Cadell, in the Strand; J. Robson, New Bond-Street; T. Durham, Charing-Cross, London; and W. Creech, Edinburgh.

Farmer, A. B. (2023). Ann Griffin: Printer and Publisher in Eliot's Court Press. In R. Stenner, K. Kramer, and A. J. Smith, eds., *The People of*

Print: Seventeenth-Century England. Cambridge: Cambridge University Press, pp. 38–44.

Feather, J. (2018). Business Models in the Eighteenth-Century London Book Trade. *Publishing History*, 78, 55–83.

  (1990). The Country Trade in Books. In R. Myers and M. Harris, eds., *Spreading the Word: the Distribution Networks of Print, 1550–1850*. Winchester: St Paul's Bibliographies, pp. 165–183.

  (1985). *The Provincial Book Trade in the Eighteenth Century*. Cambridge: Cambridge University Press.

Ferdinand, C. Y. (2004). Ann Ward (1715/16–1789). *ODNB*.

  (2004). Cesar Ward (1711–1759). *ODNB*.

Fisher, A. (1753). *A New Grammar*, 3rd ed. London: A. Fisher.

Flint, C. (2011). *The Appearance of Print in Eighteenth-Century Fiction*. Cambridge: Cambridge University Press.

Gadd, I. (2017). The Stationers' Company. In P. Sabor and B. A. Schellenberg, eds., *Samuel Richardson in Context*. Cambridge: Cambridge University Press, pp. 83–89.

Gales, W. (1787). *The History of Lady Emma Melcombe and Her Family*. Sheffield: Hartshead Press.

  (1815–1939). *Recollections*. Gales Family Papers, Southern Historical Collection, University of North Carolina.

Gardiner, W. (1838). *Music and Friends; or, Pleasant Recollections of a Dilettante*. London: Longman, Orme, Browne, and Longman; Combe and Crossley, Leicester.

Gardner, V. E. M. (2016). *The Business of News in England, 1760–1820*. Basingstoke: Palgrave.

  (2008). John White and the Development of Print Culture in the North East of England, 1711–1769. In C. Armstrong and J. Hinks, eds., *Book Trade Connections from the Seventeenth to the Twentieth Centuries*. London: British Library, pp. 71–92.

Gent, T. (1832). *The Life of Mr Thomas Gent, Printer, of York.* J. Hunter and T. Thorpe, eds. London: C. Adlard.

(1760). *The Unhappy Birth, Wicked Life, and Miserable Death of that Vile Traitor, and Apostle, Judas Iscariot.* Newcastle: John White.

Gentleman, F. (1764). *A Trip to the Moon, Containing an Account of the Island Noibla, Its Inhabitants, Religious and Political Customs, &c. by Sir Humphrey Lunatic, Bart.* York: Printed by A. Ward, for S. Crowder; W. Bristow; J. Pridden and W. Griffin; G. Burnet; G. Woodfall; and J. Johnson, London; C. Etherington, in York; and W. Charnley, in Newcastle Upon Tyne.

Goodman, I. (2020). Rogue or Respected Businesswoman? Mary Cooper and the Role of 18th-Century Trade Publishers. *Engage: Blogs from the College of Arts, Humanities and Social Sciences*, The University of Edinburgh, 18 March, www.blogs.hss.ed.ac.uk/history-of-the-book/rogue-or-respected-businesswoman-mary-cooper-and-the-role-of-18th-century-trade-publishers/.

Griffin, D. (2013). *Authorship in the Long Eighteenth Century.* Plymouth: University of Delaware Press.

Habermas, J. (1993). *The Structural Transformation of the Public Sphere: An Inquiry into a Category of Bourgeois Society.* T. Burger, trans. Cambridge: Polity Press.

Harris, J. (1723). *Lexicon Technicum: Or, an Universal England Dictionary of Arts and Sciences.* London: D. Brown, J. Walthoe, J. Knapton, B. and S. Tooke, D. Midwinter, B. Cowse, T. Ward, E. Symon, E. Valentine, and J. Clark. ESTC 006383661.

Harris, M. (1993). Literature and Commerce in Eighteenth-Century London: The Making of *The Champion*. In T. N. Corns and J. A. Downie, eds., *Telling People What to Think: Early Eighteenth-Century Periodicals from the Review to the Rambler.* London: F. Cass, pp. 94–115.

Hartopp, H., ed. (1933). *Register of the Freemen of Leicester, 1770–1930, Including the Apprentices*. Leicester: Backus.

Hartopp, H., ed. (1935). *Roll of the Mayors of the Borough and Lord Mayors of the City of Leicester, 1209–1935*. Leicester: Backus.

Hawkridge, J. (1764). *A Treatise on Fevers in General, Their Nature and Treatment*. York: printed by A. Ward, for the Author, and sold by S. Crowder, in Pater-noster-Row; W. Bristow, in St. Paul's Church-Yard; J. Pridden and W. Griffin, in Fleet-Street; G. Burnet, in the Strand; G. Woodfall, at Charing-Cross; and J. Johnson, opposite the Monument, London: C. Etherington, in York; and W. Charnley in Newcastle upon Tyne.

Hickerson, M. L. (2006). 'Ways of Lying': Anne Askew and the Examinations. *Gender and History*, 18(1), 50–65.

Hill, A. (1711). *The Book of Ecclesiastes Paraphras'd*. Newcastle: John White.

Hinks, J. (2006). The Coming of Print to Leicester. *The Leicester Historian*, 42, 3–6.

  (2020). The History of Printing and Print Culture: Contexts and Controversies. *Midland History*, 45(2), 33–44.

  (2004). John Gregory and the Leicester Journal. In B. McKay, J. Hinks, and M. Bell, eds., *Light on the Book Trade: Essays in Honour of Peter Isaac*. London: British Library, pp. 85–94.

  (2000). Some Radical Printers and Booksellers of Leicester, c.1790–1850. In P. Isaac and B. McKay, eds., *The Mighty Engine: The Printing Press and Its Impact*. Winchester: St Paul's Bibliographies, pp. 175–84.

Hinks, J. and M. Bell. (2005). The Book Trade in English Provincial Towns, 1700–1849: An Evaluation of Evidence from the British Book Trade Index. *Publishing History*, 57, 53–112.

Hitchcock, R. (1773). *The Macaroni, a Comedy: As It Is Performed at the Theatre-Royal in York*. York: Printed by A. Ward, in Coney-Street.

Hodgson, J. (1921). John Cunningham, Pastoral Poet, 1729–1773: Recollections and Some Original Letters. *Archaeologia Aeliana*, 3rd series, 18, 83–100.

Hooker, R. (1682). *The Works of that Learned and Judicious Divine, Mr. Richard Hooker*. London: Robert Scot, Thomas Basset, John Wright and Richard Chiswel. ESTC 006103892.

Hooker, R. (1723). *The Works of that Learned and Judicious Divine, Mr. Richard Hooker*. London: John Walthoe, George Conyers, James Knapton, Robert Knaplock, J. and B. Sprint, Dan. Midwinter, Bernard Lintot, Benj. Cowse, William Taylor, W. and J. Innys, John Osborne, Ranew Robinson, Sam. Tooke, Tho. Wotton.

Hughes, J. and J. E. Galliard. (1717). *Calypso and Telemachus, an Opera*. London: Printed for K. Sanger, and sold by A. Dodd at the Peacock without Temple-Bar.

Hunt, C. J. (1975). *The Book-Trade in Northumberland and Durham to 1860*. Newcastle: Thorne's.

Hunt, W. ['W.H.'] (1713). *The Fall of Tarquin: A Tragedy*. York: Printed by John White, and sold at the Star in Stone-Gate; Newcastle: John White.

Hunt, M. (1984). Hawkers, Bawlers, and Mercuries: Women and the London Press in the Early Enlightenment. In M. Hunt, M. Jacob, P. Mack, and R. Perry, eds., *Women and the Enlightenment*. London: Routledge, pp. 41–68.

Hunt, M. R. (2008). Nutt [formerly Carr], Elizabeth (b. in or before 1666, d. 1746), *ODNB*, https://doi.org/10.1093/ref:odnb/66882.

Hunt, T. L. (1996). Women's Participation in the Eighteenth-Century English Publishing Trades. *Leipziger Jahrbuch Zur Buchgeschichte*, 6, 47–65.

Immel, A. (2009). Children's Books and School-Books. In M. R. Suarez, Society of Jesus, and M. L. Turner, eds., *The Cambridge History of the*

Book in Britain, 1695–1830. Cambridge: Cambridge University Press, pp. 736–49.

Immel, A., and B. Alderson. (2013). Nurse Lovechild's Legacy: The History of *Tommy Thumb's Pretty Song-Book*. In A. Immel and B. Alderson, eds., *Tommy Thumb's Pretty Song-Book: The First Collection of English Nursery Rhymes (Facsimile edition)*. Princeton: Cotsen Occasional Press, pp. 1–79.

Ireland, A. (1789). *A Catalogue of Books, Containing a Great Variety in Most Languages, Arts, and Sciences*. Leicester: Ann Ireland.

Isaac, P. (2004). Fisher [married name Slack], Anne, (1719–1778). *ODNB*.

(2004). Thomas Slack, 1723?–1784. *ODNB*.

(1998). Thomas Slack, 1723?–1874. *Quadrat*, 7, 18–21.

Jones, C. and G. Holmes. (1985). *The London Diaries of William Nicolson, Bishop of Carlisle, 1702–1718*. Oxford: Clarendon Press.

Kay, S. and N. Kay. (2017). *How Great a Crime to Tell the Truth: The Story of Joseph and Winifred Gales and the Sheffield Register*. Sheffield: 1889 Books.

Kempis, T. à. (1689). *The Christian's Pattern: Or, a Treatise of the Imitation of Jesus Christ*. London: William Onley, M. Gillyflower, R. Sare, T. Bennet, F. Saunders, and M. Wotton. ESTC 006106452.

Lackington, J. (1792). *Memoirs of the first Forty-Five Years of the Life of James Lackington*. London.

Limouze, A. S. (1950). Doctor Gaylard's Loyal Observator Reviv'd. *Modern Philology*, 48(2), 97–103.

(1947). A Study of Nathaniel Mist's Weekly Journals. Unpublished PhD thesis, Duke University.

Mackie, E. (1997). *Market à la Mode: Fashion, Commodity and Gender in* The Tatler *and* The Spectator. Baltimore: John Hopkins Press.

Mandelbrote, G. (1997). Richard Bentley's Copies: The Ownership of Copyrights in the late Seventeenth Century. In A. Hunt, G. Mandelbrote, and A. Shell, eds., *The Book Trade and Its Customers,*

1450–1900: Historical Essays for Robin Myers. Winchester: St Paul's Bibliographies, pp. 77–94.

Manley, K. R. (2004). *'Redeeming Love Proclaim': John Rippon and the Baptists*. Carlisle: The Paternoster Press.

(2004). 'Rippon, John (1751–1836)'. *ODNB*.

Martinez, C. S., and C. E. Roman, eds. (2023). *Female Printmakers, Printsellers, and Print Publishers in the Eighteenth Century: The Imprint of Women, c. 1700–1830*. Cambridge: Cambridge University Press.

Maruca, L. (2007). *The Work of Print: Authorship and the English Text Trades, 1660–1760*. Seattle, DC: The University of Washington Press.

Mason, W. (1777). *Caractacus, a Dramatic Poem [...] Now Altered for Theatrical Representation*. York: Printed by A. Ward, and sold by R. Horsfeld and J. Dodsley in London.

Mason, W. (1778). *The Poems of Mr. Gray, to Which Are Added Memoirs of His Life and Writings*. York: Printed by A. Ward, and sold by J. Dodsley, Pall-Mall; T. Cadell, in the Strand, London; and J. Todd, York.

(1771). *Scarborough, a Poem in Three Cantoes*, 2nd ed. York: Printed by A. Ward, for W. Tesseyman [York] and sold by J. Dodsley, in Pall Mall, and Mess. Robinson and Roberts, in Pater-noster-Row, London.

Mawer, J. (1737). *Roma Meretrix*. Newcastle upon Tyne: Printed by John White; and sold by Mess. Innys and Manby in London; Mr. Bryson in Newcastle; and Mr. Hildyard and Mr. Staples in York.

McDowell, P. (1998). *The Women of Grub Street: Press, Politics, and Gender in the London Literary Marketplace, 1678–1730*. Oxford: Clarendon Press.

McKenzie, D. F. (1974). *Stationers' Company Apprentices*. Oxford: Oxford Bibliographical Society.

McKitterick, D. (2003). *Print, Manuscript, and the Search for Order, 1450–1830*. Cambridge: Cambridge University Press.

Mitchell, C. J. (1995). Women in the Eighteenth-Century Book Trades. In O. M. Brack, Jr., ed., *Writers, Books, and Trade: An Eighteenth-Century Miscellany for William B. Todd*. New York: AMS Press, pp. 25–75.

Monkman, K. (1970). The Bibliography of the Early Editions of *Tristram Shandy*. *The Library*, –XXV(1), 11–39.

Mullan, J., and C. Reid, eds. (2005). *Eighteenth-Century Popular Culture: A Selection*. Oxford: Oxford University Press.

Munby, A. N. L., and L. Coral. (1977). *British Book Sale Catalogues, 1676–1800: A Union List*. London: Mansell.

Music, D. W. (2001). Baptist Church Music. *Grove Music Online*. www.oxfordmusiconline.com.

Nebeker, E. (2011). The Broadside Ballad and Textual Publics. *Studies in English Literature* 51(1), 1–19.

Nichols, J. (1814). *Literary Anecdotes of the Eighteenth Century*. London: Nichols, Son, and Bentley.

Nicholson, J. (1695). *A Catalogue of Excellent Books in Greek, Latin, French, Italian, Spanish, English, &C*. London. ESTC 006128984.

Nutt, E. (1728). Nutt, Elizabeth, Widow, to the King. Petition to Be Discharged from a Prosecution for Selling *Mist's Journal* of 24 August 1728. Folios 249–250. MS Records Assembled by the State Paper Office SP 36/9/2 f. 100.

Oldmixon, J. (1713). *The Secret History of Europe. Part II*. London: Printed by J. Darby in Bartholomew-Close, for K. Sanger, and are to be sold by N. Cliff and D. Jackson near Mercers-Chappel in Cheapside, and J. Pemberton against St. Dunstan's Church in Fleetstreet.

Orr, L. (2018). Tactics of Publishing and Selling Fiction in the Long Eighteenth Century. *Huntington Library Quarterly*, 81(3), 399–423.

Ozment, K. (2022). What Does It Mean to Publish? A Messy Accounting of Ann Dodd. The Women's Print History Project. 5 August. https://womensprinthistoryproject.com/blog/post/111.

Patterson, A. T. (1975). *Radical Leicester: A History of Leicester 1780–1850*. Leicester: Leicester University Press.

Pearson, D. (2020). Bookbinding History and Sacred Cows. *The Library*, 21 (4), 498–517.

Pickering, S. F., Jr. (1981). *John Locke and Children's Books in Eighteenth-Century England*. Knoxville: University of Tennessee Press.

Plomer, H. R., G. H. Bushnell, and E. R. Dix. (1932). *A Dictionary of the Printers and Booksellers Who Were at Work in England, Scotland, and Ireland from 1726 to 1775*. Oxford: Bibliographical Society at the Oxford University Press.

Pollock, A. (2009). *Gender and the Fictions of the Public Sphere, 1690–1755*. London: Routledge.

Pope, A. (1743). *The Dunciad, in Four Books. Printed According to the Complete Copy Found in the Year 1742. With the Prolegomena of Scriblerus, and Notes Variorum*. London: Printed for M. Cooper at the Globe in Pater-noster-row.

Porter, R. (1987). *Disease, Medicine and Society in England, 1550–1860*. London: Macmillan.

Powell, M. (2012). *Performing Authorship in Eighteenth-Century English Periodicals*. Plymouth: Bucknell University Press.

Pyke, E. et al. (1792). *Hymns and Songs in Praise of Jesus Christ*. Leicester: Ann Ireland.

Raven, J. (2014). *Bookscape: Geographies of Printing and Publishing in London before 1800*. London: The British Library.

(2007). Britain, 1750–1830. In F. Moretti, ed., *The Novel, Volume 1*. Princeton: Princeton University Press, pp. 429–54.

(2007). *The Business of Books: Booksellers and the English Book Trade, 1450–1850*. New Haven: Yale University Press.

(2014). *Publishing Business in Eighteenth-Century England*. New York: Boydell and Brewer.

Rippon, J. (1793). *The Baptist Annual Register for 1790, 1791, 1792, and Part of 1793, Including Sketches of the State of Religion among Different Denominations of Good Men at Home and Abroad*. London: John Rippon.

  (1804). *A Discourse on the Origin and Progress of the Society for Promoting Religious Knowledge among the Poor, from Its Commencement in 1750, to the Year 1802, Including a Succinct Account of the Separate Publications in Their Catalogue, Etc*. London: John Rippon.

  (1810). *A Selection of Psalm and Hymn Tunes*. London: John Rippon.

  (1784). *A Sermon Occasioned by the Death of the Reverend Andrew Gifford, D.D. By John Rippon. With an Address Delivered at His Internment, by John Ryland*. London: John Rippon.

Rippon, J., and T. Walker. (1806). *The Selection of Tunes in Miniature [. . .] Engraved by A. Davies*. London: John Rippon.

Rivers, I. (2007). The First Evangelical Tract Society. *The Historical Journal*, 50(1), 1–22.

Rodgers, M. (2023). Deconstructing Reliance on Enlightenment Methods in Feminist Book Historical Scholarship. *Eighteenth-Century Fiction*, 35(4), 517–19.

Rodríguez-Gil, M. E. (2002). Ann Fisher: First Female Grammarian. *Historical Sociolinguistics and Sociohistorical Linguistics*, 2, unpaginated.

Rogers, P. (1985). *Literature and Popular Culture in Eighteenth-Century England*. London: Harvester Wheatsheaf.

Rogers, P., and P. Baines. (2007). Edmund Curll, Citizen and Liveryman: Politics and the Book Trade. *Publishing History*, 62, 5–39.

Rose, M. (1988). The Author as Proprietor: Donaldson v. Becket and the Genealogy of Modern Authorship. *Representations*, 23, 51–85.

Schneller, B. E. (1987). *Mary Cooper, Eighteenth-Century London Bookseller: A Bibliography*. Unpublished PhD thesis. The Catholic University of America.

Schneller, B. (2018). John Hill and Mary Cooper: A Case Study in Eighteenth-Century Publishing. In C. Brant and G. Rousseau, eds., *Fame and Fortune: Sir John Hill and London Life in the 1750s*. London: Palgrave, pp. 107–20.

(1990). Mary Cooper and Periodical Publishing, 1743–1761. *Journal of Newspaper and Periodical History*, 6(2), 31–5.

Scott, W. (1890). *The Monthly Chronicle of North-Country Lore and Legend*, Vol. 4. Newcastle upon Tyne: Published for proprietors of the Newcastle weekly chronicle by W. Scott.

Sessions, W. K., and E. M. Sessions (1976). *Printing in York: From the 1490s to the Present Day*. York: William Sessions.

Shakespeare, W., and N. Rowe. (1714). *The Works of Mr. William Shakespeare*. London: Printed for J. Tonson, E. Curll, J. Pemberton, and K. Sanger, and are to be sold by J. Knapton and D. Midwinter in St. Paul's Church-yard, A. Betsworth on London-Bridg, W. Taylor in Pater-noster-Row, T. Varnam and J. Osborn in Lombard-street, and J. Browne near Temple-Bar.

Sher, R. B. (2006). *The Enlightenment and the Book: Scottish Authors and Their Publishers in Eighteenth-Century Britain, Ireland, and America*. Chicago: University of Chicago Press.

Shirley, J. (1711). *The Famous History of the Valiant London Prentice*. Newcastle: John White.

Shrank, C. (2008). Trollers and Dreamers: Defining the Citizen-Subject in Sixteenth-Century Cheap Print. *The Yearbook of English Studies*, 38 (1–2), 102–18.

Siskin, C. (1998). *The Work of Writing: Literature and Social Change in Britain, 1799–1830*. Baltimore: Johns Hopkins.

Slack and Co. (1765). Just Published, Price Two-Pence Half-Penny, to Be Continued Weekly on the Saturday, by T. Slack, (Bookseller) and Co. A New Periodical Paper of News, Commerce, and Entertainment,

Entitled, *The Newcastle Chronicle*: Or, *General Weekly Advertiser*. Newcastle: Slack.

Smith, J. (1711). *A Sermon Preached to the Sons of the Clergy*. Newcastle: John White.

Stenner, R., K. Kramer, and A. J. Smith, eds., (2022). *Print Culture, Agency, and Regionality in the Hand Press Period*. London: Palgrave Macmillan.

Smith, J. (2001). Books and Culture in Late Eighteenth- and Early Nineteenth-century Newcastle. In P. Isaacs and B. McKay, eds., *The Moving Market: Continuity and Change in the Book Trade*. New Castle: Oak Knoll Press, pp. 1–26.

Smith, H. (2012). 'Grossly Material Things': Women and Book Production in Early Modern England. Oxford: Oxford University Press.

Smith, A. J. (2022). The Newspaper, the Bookshop, and the Radical Society: Joseph Gales' Hartshead Press and the 'Reading and Thinking People of Sheffield'. In R. Stenner, K. Kramer, and A. J. Smith, eds., *Print Culture, Agency, and Regionality in the Hand Press Period*. London: Palgrave Macmillan, pp. 71–89.

Sterne, L. (1965). *The Letters of Laurence Sterne*, L. P. Curtis, ed. Oxford: Clarendon Press.

Symonds, M. T. (2007). Grub Street Culture: The Newspapers of Nathaniel Mist, 1716–1737. Unpublished PhD thesis, University College London.

Thomas, A. (1782–6). *Observations on the Nature, Kinds, Causes, and Prevention of Insanity, Lunacy, or Madness*. Leicester: Printed by G. Ireland, for G. Robinson, and T. Cadell, London.

Thompson, J. (1871). *The History of Leicester in the Eighteenth-Century*. Leicester: Crossley and Clark.

Tillotson, J. (1720). *The Works of the Most Revered Dr. John Tillotson, Late Lord Archbishop of Caterbury*. London: Timothy Goodwin, Benjamin Tooke, John Pemberton, John Nicholson and Jacob Tonson.

Tonson, J. (1718). Assignment of Copyright: London, 17 September 1718. The Rosenbach Museum, Philadelphia, EMs 417/20.

Treadwell, M. (1982). London Trade Publishers 1675–1750. *The Library*, sixth series, 4(2), 99–134.

Trowles, T. (2012). Vincent, William (1739–1815). *ODNB*.

Vincent, W. (1790). *Considerations on Parochial Music*. London: T. Cadell.

Wayne, V., ed. (2020). *Women's Labour and the History of the Book in Early Modern England*. London: Bloomsbury.

Welford, R. (1907). Early Newcastle Typography, 1639–1800. *Archaeologia Aeliana*, third series, Vol. 3, 1–134.

Wesley, J. (1827). *The Journal of the Rev. John Wesley, A.M.*, Vol. 2. London: Published and sold by J. Kershaw.

Wigglesworth, M. (1711). *Day of Doom: A Poetical Description of the Great and Last Judgement*. Newcastle: John White.

Will of Catherine Sanger. 1 June 1731. Records of the Prerogative Court of Canterbury. National Archives, London. PROB 11.

Will of John Nicholson, Stationer of London. April 1717. National Archives, London, PROB 11/558/241.

Will of John White. January 1715/16. Prerogative and Exchequer Courts of York. Borthwick Institute for Archives, University of York.

Williams, H. (2020). The Good Humour Club or Doctors' Club and Sterne's *Political Romance*. *The Shandean*, 31, 138–55. (2022).

Printing, Publishing, and Pocket Book Compiling: Ann Fisher's Hidden Labour in the Newcastle Book Trade. In R. Stenner, K. Kramer, and A. J. Smith, eds, *Print Culture, Agency, and Regionality in the Hand Press Period*. London: Palgrave Macmillan, pp. 93–116.

Wilson, K. (1985). Citizenship, Empire and Modernity in the English Provinces, c.1720–1790. *Eighteenth-Century Studies*, 29, 69–96.

Wilson, A. (1765). *Short Remarks upon Autumnal Disorders of the Bowels*. Newcastle: John White.

Wollstonecraft, M. (2010). *The Vindication of the Rights of Woman*. Cambridge: Cambridge University Press.

Woodring, B. (2023). Ruth Raworth: Constructing Milton and Moseley. In R. Stenner, K. Kramer, and A. J. Smith, et al., *The People of Print: Seventeenth-Century England*. Cambridge: Cambridge University Press, pp. 45–52.

Yarn, M. (2023). Invisible Furniture: Women Printers in the London Book Trade. Bibliographical Society Presentation, London, 21 November.

Zaret, D. (2000). *Origins of Democratic Culture: Printing, Petitions, and the Public Sphere in Early-Modern England*. Princeton: Princeton University Press.

*This volume is dedicated to the memory of John Hinks:
friend, mentor, and scholar.*

Cambridge Elements

Publishing and Book Culture

SERIES EDITOR
Samantha J. Rayner
University College London

Samantha J. Rayner is Professor of Publishing and Book Cultures at UCL. She is also Director of UCL's Centre for Publishing, co-Director of the Bloomsbury CHAPTER (Communication History, Authorship, Publishing, Textual Editing and Reading) and co-Chair of the Bookselling Research Network.

ASSOCIATE EDITOR
Leah Tether
University of Bristol

Leah Tether is Professor of Medieval Literature and Publishing at the University of Bristol. With an academic background in medieval French and English literature and a professional background in trade publishing, Leah has combined her expertise and developed an international research profile in book and publishing history from manuscript to digital.

ADVISORY BOARD

Simone Murray, Monash University

Claire Squires, University of Stirling

Andrew Nash, University of London

Leslie Howsam, Ryerson University

David Finkelstein, University of Edinburgh

Alexis Weedon, University of Bedfordshire

Alan Staton, Booksellers Association

Angus Phillips, Oxford International Centre for Publishing

Richard Fisher, Yale University Press

John Maxwell, Simon Fraser University

Shafquat Towheed, The Open University

Jen McCall, Central European University Press/ Amsterdam University Press

ABOUT THE SERIES

This series aims to fill the demand for easily accessible, quality texts available for teaching and research in the diverse and dynamic fields of Publishing and Book Culture. Rigorously researched and peer-reviewed Elements will be published under themes, or 'Gatherings'. These Elements should be the first check point for researchers or students working on that area of publishing and book trade history and practice: we hope that, situated so logically at Cambridge University Press, where academic publishing in the UK began, it will develop to create an unrivalled space where these histories and practices can be investigated and preserved.

Cambridge Elements

Publishing and Book History

Gathering Editor: Andrew Nash

Andrew Nash is Reader in Book History and Director of the London Rare Books School at the Institute of English Studies, University of London. He has written books on Scottish and Victorian Literature, and edited or co-edited numerous volumes including, most recently, *The Cambridge History of the Book in Britain, Volume 7* (Cambridge University Press, 2019).

Gathering Editor: Leah Tether

Leah Tether is Professor of Medieval Literature and Publishing at the University of Bristol. With an academic background in medieval French and English literature and a professional background in trade publishing, Leah has combined her expertise and developed an international research profile in book and publishing history from manuscript to digital.

ELEMENTS IN THE GATHERING

Publication and the Papacy in Late Antique and Medieval Europe
Samu Niskanen

Publishing in Wales: Renaissance and Resistance
Jacob D. Rawlins

The People of Print: Seventeenth-Century England
Rachel Stenner, Kaley Kramer and Adam James Smith *et al.*

Publishing in a Medieval Monastery: The View from Twelfth-Century Engelberg
Benjamin Pohl

Communicating the News in Early Modern Europe
Jenni Hyde, Massimo Rospocher, Joad Raymond, Yann Ryan, Hannu Salmi and Alexandra Schäfer-Griebel

Printing Technologies and Book Production in Seventeenth-Century Japan
Peter Kornicki

Unprinted: Publication Beyond the Press
Daria Kohler and Daniel Wakelin *et al.*

Mudie's Select Library and the Shelf Life of the Nineteenth-Century Novel
Karen Wade

Transnational Crusoe, Illustration and Reading History, 1719–1722
Sandro Jung

Art Books for the People: The Origins of The Penguin Modern Painters
David Trigg

Pamphleteering: Polemic, Print, and the Infrastructure of Political Agency
Pierre-Héli Monot

The People of Print: Eighteenth-Century England
Adam James Smith, Rachel Stenner and Kaley Kramer *et al.*

A full series listing is available at: www.cambridge.org/EPBC

For EU product safety concerns, contact us at Calle de José Abascal, 56–1°,
28003 Madrid, Spain or eugpsr@cambridge.org.

www.ingramcontent.com/pod-product-compliance
Lightning Source LLC
LaVergne TN
LVHW011843060526
838200LV00054B/4148